THE BEST HOLIDAYS EVER

FROM THE NESTLÉ KITCHEN

A NESTLÉ CANADA INC.
QUANTUM BOOK

Nestlé

Canadian Cataloguing in Publication Data

The best holidays ever

Published also in French under title: Délices du temps des fêtes.
"A Nestlé Canada Inc/Quantum book."
Includes index.
ISBN 1-895892-06-6

1. Christmas cookery.   2. Entertaining.
I. Nestlé Canada Inc.

TX739.2.C45B47 1996   641.5'66   C96-931330-6

Editorial Director:	Hugh Brewster
Project Editor:	Wanda Nowakowska
Editorial Assistance:	Beverley Renahan
Production Director:	Susan Barrable
Production Coordinator:	Sandra L. Hall
Book Design and Layout:	Gordon Sibley Design Inc.
Color Separation:	Colour Technologies
Printing and Binding:	Friesens Corporation

Cover photo: Berry Good Parfaits (p.40)

THE BEST HOLIDAYS EVER
was produced by Madison Press Books,
which is under the direction of
Albert E. Cummings

Produced for The Quantum Book Group Inc.
149 Lowther Avenue, Toronto, Ontario, Canada M5R 3M5

Printed and bound in Canada

CONTENTS

Decadent Truffle Squares (p.13)

Alfredo Natasha (p.27)

Christmas Cranberry Dessert (p.43)

Northern Sunset (p.77)

Welcome to the Most Wonderful Time of the Year

I absolutely love Christmas holidays — especially the sharing of favorite foods with the special people in my life. But dishes that are rich in tradition can also be rich in calories! That's why I'm delighted to see that Nestlé Canada Inc. has included nutritional analysis and information for all the appetizing recipes you'll find in this beautiful and practical holiday cookbook.

The holidays come only once a year, and THE BEST HOLIDAYS EVER will help you make the most of every minute — and every entertaining occasion. Helpful menu ideas and serving suggestions, plus over 100 great-tasting and easy-to-make recipes, guarantee that your holidays will be healthy, happy and relaxed.

I congratulate Nestlé Canada Inc. for their generous support of Kids Help Phone. I'm honored to be associated with this cookbook, and hope that you'll add your support to it.

Happy holidays!

Anne Lindsay

Anne Lindsay
Cookbook Author
and Nutritionist

With presents to wrap, pageants to attend, and parties for family and friends, there isn't a lot of extra time to spend in the kitchen during the holidays.

At Nestlé, we understand the dreams — and the demands! — that make up the magic of Christmas each year. We've built our reputation on deliciously easy recipes and timesaving shortcuts for today's busy cooks. Now, in THE BEST HOLIDAYS EVER, we've compiled all the cherished Nestlé recipes that cooks across Canada have come to depend on year after year — plus dozens of exciting new dishes that are sure to make this holiday especially memorable. Lots of make-ahead recipes, shopping tips, menu suggestions and cooking shortcuts are also included to help you through the holidays with ease and style.

But that's not the only reason we're calling THE BEST HOLIDAYS EVER an invaluable holiday cope-book. We're also helping a very important Canadian charity, Kids Help Phone — and so are you!

Five dollars ($5.00) from the sale of every book goes directly to Kids Help Phone to help this important charity continue its critical work with children right across the country. Nestlé Canada Inc. is proud to be a founding sponsor of Kids Help Phone and to be involved with them in this exciting fundraising project.

From our kitchen to yours, our warmest wishes for the best holidays ever!

Marilyn Knox
Senior Vice President, Corporate Affairs
Nestlé Canada Inc.

The holiday season is assumed to be — and should be — a time of wonderment, joy and thanksgiving for families, friends and communities. Unfortunately, thousands of children do not have that special circle of family or friends. For some, it is a time when family problems can seem overwhelming, especially when compared to the high expectations so commonly associated with the holiday season.

Kids Help Phone knows these realities all too well. As Canada's only national toll-free, 24-hour helpline for children and youth, we answer 1,500 calls every day. And the holiday season is no exception. Messages of confusion, loneliness, isolation, fear and depression flood our telephone lines.

Kids Help Phone has been proud to have Nestlé Canada Inc. as a founding sponsor. Each year, Nestlé employees, in partnership with our fundraising team, have developed wonderfully creative ways to raise public awareness and much needed funds for this vital service. This year is no exception and, in fact, THE BEST HOLIDAYS EVER cookbook may be Nestlé's best fundraising idea ever.

Your purchase of this quality cookbook will no doubt bring further enjoyment to your holiday activities. In addition, though, you will be helping a child who is painfully aware of the festivities this holiday brings to other children.

I wish you, your family and friends a joyous holiday season and thank you for supporting Kids Help Phone.

Heather Sproule
National Executive Director
Kids Help Phone/Jeunesse, J'écoute

COUNTDOWN

Let our handy Holiday Planner help you get a head start on planning and preparing for the holidays this year. From stocking the pantry to filling the stockings, we'll show you just how easy it is to have the best holidays ever — this year, and every year after!

6 WEEKS to Go

- Plan menus for holiday entertaining.
- Make list of candies, cookies and cakes to make for gift giving (see Chapter One). Stock up on decorative boxes, tins and jars plus tissue, cellophane and ribbon (see p.10).
- Make and freeze dough for **Giant Turtles Treasure Cookies** (p.17). These chewy, butterscotchy cookies are perfect stocking stuffers or sweet treats for the younger crowd (adults will love them, too!).
- Stock the pantry (see p.53). Purchase alcoholic and nonalcoholic beverages, napkins, extra glasses.
- Send out party invitations.
- Organize Cookie and Candy Exchange for first Saturday of December.
- Unpack holiday decorations. Check Christmas lights. Replenish stock of candles.
- Start food hamper for neighborhood food bank.
- Plant paperwhites and other bulbs indoors for forcing. Buy extra bulbs and containers for gift giving.

5 WEEKS to Go

- Start shopping for gifts (see Chapter Four for quick-to-make weeknight meals).
- Prepare **Pancake Quick Mix** (p.63) and **Basic Muffin Mix** (p.66) to have on hand for holiday breakfasts.

4 WEEKS to Go

- Bake and freeze **Light Fruitcake** (p.18), **Cranberry Mincemeat Loaves** (p.18) and **Cherry Pound Cake** (p.46). Make and freeze **Caramel Nut Bouchée** (p.10).
- Host Cookie and Candy Exchange (see box, p.10 for tips on packaging).
- Mail Christmas cards overseas.

3 WEEKS to Go

- Set aside a weekend afternoon with the family and make delightful **Peanut Truffle Mice** (p.15). These appealing critters are as much fun to make as they are to eat!

- Let kids make their own wrapping and packaging for gifts. Set out brown paper, stencils, brightly colored markers and paints, holiday glitter, glue, old Christmas cards for cutting up — and let their imaginations do the rest!
- Make and freeze **Espresso-Chip Ice Cream Terrine** (p.37).
- Mail Christmas cards to the United States.

2 WEEKS to Go

- Make and freeze **Toffee Mini Tarts** (p.10).
- Organize a family outing to a local cut-your-own Christmas tree farm. Afterwards, warm up with big bowlfuls of **Hot and Spicy Bean Pot** (p.70).
- Start wrapping gifts.

to the HOLIDAYS!

* Welcome the young crowd to an afternoon of assembling and decorating luscious Christmas houses made of Nestlé Kit Kat candy bars — and other candy delights! (Nestlé Kit Kat Candy Craft Cabins are available at seasonal candy displays in drug and select stores across the country.)
* Mail Christmas cards within Canada.

1 WEEK *to Go*

* Make and refrigerate **Brandy Toffee Sauce** (p.38) and **Velvety Fudge Sauce** (p.39). Make extra and store in decorative jars for last-minute hostess gifts or stocking stuffers.
* Make and package **Deliciously Decadent Truffle Squares** (p.13), **Five-Minute Fudge** (p.17) and **White Chocolate and Cherry Fudge** (p.14) for the chocolate lovers on your list. Remember to keep refrigerated.
* Invite friends for an evening of carols and holiday cheer. Let them nibble on **Grilled Chicken Ribbons** (p.24) and **Nippy Cheddar Spread** (p.74) with crackers while you heat up **Mulled Citrus and Spice Tea** (p.77).

* Deliver holiday hamper to food bank.
* Whip up a large bowlful of **Nescafé Coffeenog** (p.33) to enjoy while trimming the tree.
* Help your child wrap up some **Peanut Truffle Mice** (p.15) in a pretty gift box to give to teacher on the last day of school.
* Invite neighbors over for coffee and **Luscious Turtles Cheesecake** (p.46).

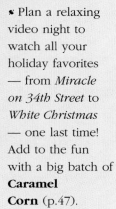

CHRISTMAS EVE

* Prepare **Make-Ahead Baked French Toast** (p.62) for breakfast on Christmas morning.
* Assemble and refrigerate **Light Cranberry-Orange Trifle** (p.43) to serve with the Christmas Feast.
* After the last of the stockings has been stuffed, relax by the fire with a decidedly grown-up **Orange Truffle Hot Chocolate** (p.33).

THE BIG DAY IS HERE!

* Relax and enjoy it with family and friends.

THE WEEK AFTER

* Invite friends for Saturday brunch. The night before, make and refrigerate **Italian Vegetable Strata** (p.60).
* Plan a relaxing video night to watch all your holiday favorites — from *Miracle on 34th Street* to *White Christmas* — one last time! Add to the fun with a big batch of **Caramel Corn** (p.47).
* Gather the gang for a day of skiing, skating or tobogganing, then head back for a warming bowlful of **Pantry Seafood Chowder** (p.53) or **Tex-Mex Chili Soup** (p.73). If appetites are hearty, add some corn chips and our zesty **Mexican Dip Duo** (p.76).

NEW YEAR'S EVE

* Plan a special dinner just for the two of you. Start with easy but extravagant **Alfredo Natasha** (p.27), then bring the warmth of India to the dinner table with exotic **Curried Chicken** (p.30). As the clock strikes twelve, enjoy **Frozen Tiramisu for Two** (p.36) and **Irish Coffee Cream** (p.33).

GIFTS FROM THE KITCHEN

There's no better way to say

"Happy Holidays!" to the special

people on your list than with a

beautifully packaged gift of homemade

chocolates, cookies, candies or fruitcake.

And even if you've never made

a truffle or think you just don't have the

time to bake, we've kept our recipes

simple and the ingredient lists short —

so it's both easy and fun to make

delicious gifts from your kitchen.

Clockwise from top right: Caramel Almond Bites (p.11),
Caramel Nut Bouchée (p.10), Chewy Caramel
Nut Drops (p.11), Toffee Mini Tarts (p.10). In box (from left):
Meringue Chews (p.16), Caramel Nut Bouchée,
Crunchy Bonbon (p.13), Fudgy Rolo Brownie (p.16).

CARAMEL NUT BOUCHÉE

If you like the idea of homemade candy but not the work involved, these luscious soft caramels are the perfect solution — especially during the busy holiday season (photo, p.9).

Smack wrapped toffee on counter to break bars. Unwrap; place in 4-cup (1 L) microwaveable glass measure or bowl. Add evaporated milk and butter; microwave at High for 1-1/2 to 2 minutes or until bubbling vigorously. Stir until smooth.

• Stir in coarsely chopped pecans, hazelnuts and pine nuts. Refrigerate for about 1 hour or until chilled and firm enough to handle.

• Roll slightly rounded teaspoonfuls (5 mL) into small balls; roll in finely chopped pecans. Place in small foil or paper candy cups; refrigerate for 2 hours or until firm. *(Candies can be layered between waxed paper and refrigerated in airtight container for up to 1 week or frozen for up to 4 weeks.)* Makes 25 candies.

PER CANDY: 82 CALORIES, 1 G PROTEIN, 6 G FAT, 6 G CARBOHYDRATE

3	BARS (56 G EACH) MACKINTOSH'S CREAMY TOFFEE	3
2 TBSP	CARNATION EVAPORATED MILK	25 ML
1 TSP	BUTTER	5 ML
1/2 CUP	COARSELY CHOPPED PECANS	125 ML
1/4 CUP	HAZELNUTS	50 ML
1/4 CUP	TOASTED PINE NUTS	50 ML
1/2 CUP	FINELY CHOPPED PECANS	125 ML

TOFFEE MINI TARTS

Who can resist these delectable clusters of nuts under a jewel-like toffee glaze (photo, p.9)? For extra convenience, use ready-made frozen tart shells.

Smack wrapped toffee on counter to break bars. Unwrap; place in 4-cup (1 L) microwaveable glass measure or bowl. Add evaporated milk and butter; microwave at High for 3 minutes or until bubbling vigorously. Stir until smooth. Stir in pecans, hazelnuts and almonds.

• Spoon evenly into tart shells. Refrigerate for 1 hour or until filling is set. *(Tarts can stored in single layer in airtight container and refrigerated for up to 1 week or frozen for up to 3 weeks.)* Makes 34 tarts.

PER TART: 163 CALORIES, 2 G PROTEIN, 11 G FAT, 14 G CARBOHYDRATE

6	BARS (56 G EACH) MACKINTOSH'S CREAMY TOFFEE	6
1/4 CUP	CARNATION EVAPORATED MILK	50 ML
1 TBSP	BUTTER	15 ML
1 CUP	CHOPPED PECANS	250 ML
1/2 CUP	HAZELNUTS	125 ML
1/4 CUP	TOASTED SLIVERED ALMONDS OR PINE NUTS	50 ML
34	BAKED 2-INCH (5 CM) TART SHELLS	34

PACKAGING COOKIES AND CANDIES

Here are some pretty ways to package and present the very best from your kitchen.

• Decorated cookie tins and greeting card boxes with plastic lids make ideal containers for cookies or chocolates. Be sure to layer cookies or candies with waxed paper.

• Line an inexpensive basket with tissue paper and fill with treats. Overwrap with festive cellophane and tie with ribbon. Add sprigs of greenery, if you like.

• Small lacquered boxes or dainty glass dishes are perfect for a few truffles or pieces of fudge.

• Fill old-fashioned mason jars with treats and decorate with holiday stickers, ribbons and ornaments.

CARAMEL ALMOND BITES

A cross between a candy and a cookie, these delicious caramel confections are sure to become a Christmas tradition. To add to the visual appeal, use a mix of toasted and untoasted almonds.

25	SQUARE GRAHAM CRACKERS	
6	BARS (56 G EACH) MACKINTOSH'S CREAMY TOFFEE	
2 TBSP	CARNATION EVAPORATED MILK	25 ML
2 TSP	BUTTER	10 ML
1 CUP	TOASTED SLICED ALMONDS	250 ML

Line 13-1/4- x 9-1/4-inch (33.5 cm x 23.5 cm) jelly roll pan with foil, leaving overhang over edges. Arrange graham crackers over bottom, cutting with serrated knife to fit and minimizing any gaps between crackers. Set aside.

• Smack wrapped toffee on counter to break bars. Unwrap; place in 4-cup (1 L) microwaveable glass measure or bowl. Add evaporated milk and butter; microwave at High for 3 minutes or until bubbling vigorously. Stir until smooth.

• Pour over graham crackers, spreading as evenly and as close to cracker edges as possible without going over edges. Sprinkle almonds evenly over top; press in gently. Refrigerate for 1 hour or until firm.

• Grasp foil and lift from pan. Using sharp knife, cut into 1-inch (2.5 cm) squares; peel off foil. *(Chilled squares can be layered between waxed paper in airtight container and refrigerated for up to 1 week. Let come to room temperature before serving.)* Makes 117 pieces.

PER PIECE: 23 CALORIES, 0.5 G PROTEIN, 1 G FAT, 3 G CARBOHYDRATE

CHEWY CARAMEL NUT DROPS

To present these with extra pizzazz, wrap chilled candies individually in cellophane and tie ends with ribbon like a Christmas cracker (see photo, below).

6	BARS (56 G EACH) MACKINTOSH'S CREAMY TOFFEE	6
1 TBSP	CARNATION EVAPORATED MILK	15 ML
1 TSP	BUTTER	5 ML
1 CUP	CHOPPED PECANS	250 ML
1/2 CUP	HAZELNUTS	125 ML
1/2 CUP	TOASTED PINE NUTS	125 ML

Line baking sheet with parchment paper; set aside.

• Smack wrapped toffee on counter to break bars. Unwrap; place in 4-cup (1 L) microwaveable glass measure or bowl. Add evaporated milk and butter; microwave at High for 3 minutes or until bubbling vigorously. Stir until smooth. Stir in pecans, hazelnuts and pine nuts.

• Drop by tablespoonfuls (15 mL) onto prepared baking sheet. Refrigerate for 1 hour or until firm. Place in small foil or paper candy cups, or wrap in cellophane and tie with ribbon. *(Candies can be layered between waxed paper in airtight container and refrigerated for up to 1 week. Let come to room temperature before serving.)* Makes 25 candies.

PER CANDY: 133 CALORIES, 2 G PROTEIN, 9 G FAT, 11 G CARBOHYDRATE

DELICIOUSLY DECADENT TRUFFLE SQUARES

We've taken all the work out of making luscious chocolate truffles but kept in every bit of extravagant flavor. There's no need for time-consuming rolling — just cut the truffles into squares. For the perfect hostess gift, place each truffle square in a candy cup and nestle in a decorative gift box.

1 CUP	CARNATION EVAPORATED MILK	250 ML
1/2 CUP	GRANULATED SUGAR	125 ML
2	PKG (300 G EACH) SEMISWEET CHOCOLATE CHIPS	2
1/4 CUP	LIQUEUR	50 ML
	NESTLÉ QUIK INSTANT CHOCOLATE DRINK MIX OR ICING SUGAR	

Line 9-inch (2.5 L) square cake pan with foil; set aside.

• In medium heavy saucepan, combine evaporated milk and sugar; cook over medium heat, stirring, until mixture comes to full boil. Boil for 3 minutes, stirring constantly; remove from heat.

• Add chocolate chips and liqueur; stir vigorously until chocolate is melted and smoothly combined. Pour into prepared pan.

• Refrigerate for 2 to 3 hours or until firm. Cut into 1-inch (2.5 cm) squares. Toss squares in chocolate drink mix until coated. Place in foil or paper candy cups and keep refrigerated until just before serving. *(Squares can be layered between waxed paper in airtight container and refrigerated for up to 1 week.)* Makes 80 squares.

TIP: *For a nonalcoholic version, substitute hot strong coffee made with Nescafé Rich Blend Instant Coffee or Nescafé Instant Espresso for the liqueur.*

PER SQUARE: 59 CALORIES, 1 G PROTEIN, 3 G FAT, 6 G CARBOHYDRATE, 0.5 G ALCOHOL

CRUNCHY BONBONS

Inspired by a Jacques Pépin recipe, these unbelievably easy-to-make chocolates are ready in just four minutes and will delight both the novice and the experienced candy maker.

4	BARS (44 G EACH) NESTLÉ CRUNCH CANDY	4
	TOPPINGS (SELECTION)	
	BLUEBERRIES, SLICES OF KUMQUAT, RASPBERRIES, DICED DRIED APRICOTS, RAISINS	
	HAZELNUTS, PECANS, WALNUTS, CASHEWS OR OTHER NUTS	

Unwrap and break candy bars into chunks. Place in 2-cup (500 mL) microwaveable glass measure or bowl; microwave at Medium, stirring once, for 1 minute or just until melted.

• Divide evenly among 20 small foil or paper candy cups. Arrange desired fruits or nuts on top. Refrigerate for 30 minutes or until firm; let come to room temperature before serving. Makes 20 candies.

PER CANDY: 64 CALORIES, 1 G PROTEIN, 4 G FAT, 6 G CARBOHYDRATE

TIP: *For larger candies, use twelve 2-inch (5 cm) paper muffin cups. Makes 12 candies.*

◄ Deliciously Decadent Truffle Squares

WHITE CHOCOLATE AND CHERRY FUDGE

*Classic fudge goes festive in a smooth and creamy white chocolate confection
studded with luscious candied cherries. For an extra treat, make this version as well as our popular Five-Minute Fudge
(p.17) and arrange contrasting squares on a pretty glass dish — or layer and package in holiday boxes and tins.*

Line 8-inch (2 L) square cake pan with foil; set aside.

• In large heavy saucepan, combine sugar, evaporated milk and butter; cook over medium heat, stirring, until mixture comes to full boil. Boil for 5 minutes, stirring constantly; reduce heat to low.

• Add white chocolate; stir until completely melted. Remove from heat.

• Add marshmallows; stir vigorously until melted and smoothly combined. Stir in cherries. Pour into prepared pan. Refrigerate for 1 to 2 hours or until firm. Cut into 1-inch (2.5 cm) squares. *(Fudge can be refrigerated in airtight container for up to 1 week.)* Makes 64 pieces.

PER PIECE: 62 CALORIES, 1 G PROTEIN, 2 G FAT, 10 G CARBOHYDRATE

1-2/3 CUPS	GRANULATED SUGAR	400 ML
2/3 CUP	CARNATION EVAPORATED MILK	150 ML
2 TBSP	BUTTER	25 ML
9 OZ	WHITE CHOCOLATE (9 SQUARES)	270 G
2 CUPS	MINIATURE MARSHMALLOWS	500 ML
1 CUP	HALVED RED GLACÉ CHERRIES (NOT MARASCHINO)	250 ML

PEANUT TRUFFLE MICE

Who can resist these delightful Christmas critters, peeking out from a gaily wrapped box and inviting a nibble? They're a treat to eat and just as much fun to make. Why not set aside an afternoon with the family and get everyone involved in making the most delectable of Christmas Eve mice!

1 CUP	CARNATION EVAPORATED MILK	250 ML
1/2 CUP	GRANULATED SUGAR	125 ML
2	PKG (300 G EACH) PEANUT BUTTER CHIPS	2
86	BLANCHED WHOLE ALMONDS, TOASTED (ABOUT 1/2 CUP/125 ML)	86
	UNSALTED PEANUT HALVES, SLICED ALMONDS OR SLICED HAZELNUTS	
	MELTED CHOCOLATE GARNISH (SEE BOX, ABOVE), OPTIONAL	

TIP: *For timesaving truffles, spread melted peanut butter-chip mixture into foil-lined 9-inch (2.5 L) square cake pan instead of forming into mice. Refrigerate for 1 to 2 hours or until firm. Cut into 1-inch (2.5 cm) squares. Makes 80 pieces.*

In medium heavy saucepan, combine evaporated milk and sugar; cook over medium heat, stirring, until mixture comes to full boil. Boil for 3 minutes, stirring constantly; remove from heat.

• Add peanut butter chips; stir vigorously until melted and smoothly combined. Pour into bowl; cover and refrigerate for about 1 hour or until firm.

• Shape teaspoonfuls (5 mL) of peanut butter-chip mixture into balls. Indent thumbprint into each ball and place almond inside; press mixture around almond to form egg shape. Place on waxed paper-lined sheet and press base to flatten slightly. Insert peanut halves for ears.

• Cover and refrigerate for about 1 hour or until firm. Decorate or coat with Melted Chocolate Garnish, if desired. *(Truffles can be refrigerated in single layer in airtight container for up to 1 week or frozen for up to 3 weeks.)* Makes 86 truffles.

PER TRUFFLE: 55 CALORIES, 2 G PROTEIN, 3 G FAT, 5 G CARBOHYDRATE

FUDGY ROLO BROWNIES

There's nothing more satisfying than deep, dark, deliciously fudgy brownies bursting with bitefuls of creamy caramel. Who would ever guess they owe their rich flavor to a packet of instant espresso! Keep this easy recipe on hand for last-minute hostess gifts — or to serve with after-dinner coffee by the fire.

Generously grease 8-inch (2 L) square cake pan with shortening; set aside. In bowl, mix instant espresso with amount of water required by brownie mix; set aside.

• Prepare brownie mix as directed, stirring in instant espresso mixture instead of water. Pour half into prepared pan. Arrange whole candies evenly over batter. Spoon remaining batter over each candy to cover; gently smooth top. Bake according to brownie mix directions. Let cool. Cut into 36 pieces. Makes 36 brownies.

Per Brownie (made with 400 g mix): 62 Calories, 1 g Protein, 2 g Fat, 10 g Carbohydrate

TIP: *To prevent brownies from sticking, grease pan generously with shortening (even if using nonstick pan).*

1	SACHET (1.5 G) NESCAFÉ INSTANT ESPRESSO	1
1	PKG (400 TO 450 G) BROWNIE MIX	1
1	PKG (52 G) NESTLÉ ROLO CANDY	1

MERINGUE CHEWS

These low-fat cookies will please everyone who prefers a soft and chewy meringue rather than a crispy one. For a pretty finish, dust cookies with icing sugar after they cool.

Line baking sheets with parchment paper; set aside.

• In small bowl, combine egg white with 1/2 tsp (2 mL) instant espresso; let stand for 5 minutes. Beat at high speed until frothy; gradually beat in sugar, a little at a time, until stiff peaks form. Beat in vanilla; fold in chopped candy bar and 1/2 cup (125 mL) dried apricots.

• Drop by rounded teaspoonfuls (5 mL) onto prepared sheets, leaving about 1 inch (2.5 cm) between each. Dust lightly with cinnamon or additional instant espresso. Garnish with diced dried apricots.

• Bake in 375°F (190°C) oven for 8 to 10 minutes or until lightly browned. Let cool slightly on baking sheets; remove to rack to cool completely. Makes 20 cookies.

Per cookie: 41 Calories, 1 g Protein, 1 g Fat, 7 g Carbohydrate

1	EGG WHITE	1
1/2 TSP	(APPROX) NESCAFÉ INSTANT ESPRESSO	2 ML
1/4 CUP	GRANULATED SUGAR	50 ML
1/4 TSP	VANILLA	1 ML
2	BARS (44 G EACH) NESTLÉ CRUNCH CANDY, CHOPPED	2
1/2 CUP	(APPROX) DICED DRIED APRICOTS, CRANBERRIES, RAISINS OR CANDIED FRUIT	125 ML
	GROUND CINNAMON	

GIANT TURTLES TREASURE COOKIES

*For Turtles lovers everywhere, here's the terrific taste of Turtles chocolates
in a deliciously chewy, butterscotchy cookie that will have everyone asking for more! To save time,
make batches of the dough ahead, wrap tightly and freeze until needed.*

2-1/4 CUPS	ALL-PURPOSE FLOUR	550 ML
1 TSP	EACH BAKING SODA AND SALT	5 ML
1 CUP	BUTTER, SOFTENED	250 ML
3/4 CUP	GRANULATED SUGAR	175 ML
3/4 CUP	PACKED BROWN SUGAR	175 ML
1 TSP	VANILLA	5 ML
2	EGGS	2
1 CUP	CHOPPED PECANS	250 ML
20	TURTLES CANDIES	20

TIPS: *For best results, chill dough
thoroughly before shaping into cookies.*
*• If cookie edges are getting too brown,
reduce oven temperature to 350°F (180°C)
and bake for 15 to 20 minutes.*

In small bowl, stir together flour, baking soda and salt.

• In large bowl, beat together butter, granulated sugar, brown sugar and vanilla until fluffy. Beat in eggs, one at a time, beating well after each addition. Gradually beat in flour mixture. Stir in pecans.

• Turn dough onto sheet of plastic wrap. Wrap tightly and refrigerate for 2 hours or until firm. *(Wrapped dough can be refrigerated for up to 3 days or frozen for up to 8 weeks; thaw in refrigerator before continuing with recipe.)*

• Cut into 8 equal wedges. Working with 2 wedges at a time and keeping remaining dough covered and refrigerated, form each wedge into ball; place each on sheet of plastic wrap. Using lightly floured hand, flatten balls into 6-inch (15 cm) circles; lift one with wrap and transfer to ungreased baking sheet. Peel off wrap.

• Arrange 5 Turtles on top of circle on baking sheet, 1 in center and remaining 4 around edge. Cover with second circle of dough; peel off wrap. Press edges together gently to seal. Bake in 375°F (190°C) oven for 12 to 15 minutes or until golden brown. Let cool on baking sheet for 10 minutes; transfer to rack to cool completely.

• Repeat with remaining chilled dough to make 3 more cookies. Bake and cool as above. Cut each cookie into 8 wedges to serve. Makes 4 large cookies, 8 servings per cookie.

PER SERVING: 244 CALORIES, 3 G PROTEIN, 12 G FAT, 31 G CARBOHYDRATE

FIVE-MINUTE FUDGE

*With holiday baking on every cook's mind, there's no better time to make up a
batch of this ever-popular Canadian classic.*

1-2/3 CUPS	GRANULATED SUGAR	400 ML
2/3 CUP	CARNATION EVAPORATED MILK	150 ML
2 TBSP	BUTTER	25 ML
1/2 TSP	SALT	2 ML
2 CUPS	MINIATURE MARSHMALLOWS	500 ML
1-1/2 CUPS	SEMISWEET CHOCOLATE CHIPS	375 ML
1/2 CUP	CHOPPED WALNUTS	125 ML
1 TSP	VANILLA	5 ML

Line 8-inch (2 L) square cake pan with foil; set aside.

• In large heavy saucepan, combine sugar, evaporated milk, butter and salt; cook over medium heat, stirring, until mixture comes to full boil. Boil for 5 minutes, stirring constantly; remove from heat.

• Add marshmallows, chocolate chips, nuts and vanilla; stir vigorously until marshmallows are melted and smoothly combined. Pour into prepared pan.

• Refrigerate for 1 to 2 hours or until firm. Cut into 1-inch (2.5 cm) squares. *(Fudge can be refrigerated in airtight container for up to 1 week.)* Makes 64 pieces.

PER PIECE: 62 CALORIES, 1 G PROTEIN, 2 G FAT, 10 G CARBOHYDRATE

CRANBERRY MINCEMEAT LOAVES

*Two Christmas flavor favorites team up with calcium-rich skim milk powder in a festive loaf that's
both delicious and nutritious. For a welcome hostess gift, bake miniature loaves (see variation, below), then wrap in
clear or colored cellophane and tie with a pretty holiday ribbon.*

Grease two 8-1/2- x 4-1/2-inch (1.5 L) loaf pans; set aside.

• In large bowl, cream together butter and sugar until light and fluffy.
Beat in eggs, one at a time, beating well after each addition. Beat in
orange rind and vanilla. Stir in mincemeat.

• Stir together flour, skim milk powder, baking powder, baking soda
and salt. Add to mincemeat mixture; stir until well combined. Stir in
cranberries and walnuts. Turn into prepared pans.

• Bake in 300°F (150°C) oven for 65 to 70 minutes or until cake tester
inserted in center comes out clean. Let cool in pans for 15 minutes.
Remove from pans to racks; let cool completely. Makes 2 loaves,
18 slices each.

Per slice: 156 Calories, 3 g Protein, 4 g Fat, 27 g Carbohydrate

VARIATION

• Mini Loaves: Divide batter evenly among 8 greased
5- x 3-inch (250 mL) loaf pans; bake for 60 to 65 minutes.

1/4 CUP	BUTTER, SOFTENED	50 ML
3/4 CUP	PACKED BROWN SUGAR	175 ML
2	EGGS	2
1 TBSP	GRATED ORANGE RIND	15 ML
1 TSP	VANILLA	5 ML
1	JAR (750 ML) PREPARED MINCEMEAT	1
2-1/2 CUPS	ALL-PURPOSE FLOUR	625 ML
1 CUP	CARNATION INSTANT SKIM MILK POWDER	250 ML
1/2 TSP	EACH BAKING POWDER AND BAKING SODA	2 ML
1/4 TSP	SALT	1 ML
1 CUP	COARSELY CHOPPED FRESH CRANBERRIES	250 ML
1 CUP	CHOPPED WALNUTS	250 ML

LIGHT FRUITCAKE

*Easier to make than traditional fruitcake, our timesaving cake doesn't need aging to bring out
all its wonderful flavors. Use your largest bowl to combine the batter.*

Grease and flour 10-inch (3 L) bundt pan or 9-inch (3 L) tube pan;
set aside.

• In large bowl, stir together flour, baking powder and salt. Add raisins,
almonds, pineapple, cherries and candied peel; toss together to coat.

• In very large bowl, beat butter with sugar until light and fluffy; beat in
eggs, one at a time, beating well after each addition. Beat in evaporated
milk and almond extract. Stir in flour mixture, one-third at a time, until
well blended. Turn into prepared pan.

• Bake in 250°F (120°C) oven for 2 to 2-1/2 hours or until cake tester
inserted in center comes out clean, covering loosely with foil halfway
through baking if browning too much. Let cool in pan on rack for
10 minutes. Remove from pan; let cool completely. *(Fruitcake can be
wrapped tightly and frozen for up to 1 month.)* Makes 35 thin slices.

Per slice: 321 Calories, 4 g Protein, 13 g Fat, 47 g Carbohydrate

3 CUPS	ALL-PURPOSE FLOUR	750 ML
1 TSP	BAKING POWDER	5 ML
1/2 TSP	SALT	2 ML
2-1/2 CUPS	GOLDEN RAISINS	625 ML
1-1/2 CUPS	SLIVERED ALMONDS	375 ML
1 CUP	CANDIED PINEAPPLE CHUNKS	250 ML
1 CUP	HALVED GLACÉ CHERRIES	250 ML
1 CUP	DICED MIXED CANDIED PEEL	250 ML
1-1/2 CUPS	BUTTER, SOFTENED	375 ML
1-1/2 CUPS	GRANULATED SUGAR	375 ML
6	EGGS	6
1/2 CUP	CARNATION EVAPORATED MILK	125 ML
1/2 TSP	ALMOND EXTRACT	2 ML

Cranberry Mincemeat Loaves ➤

FESTIVE ENTERTAINING

We've put the pleasure

back into holiday entertaining with a

dazzling collection of effortless recipes

that will delight guest and host alike.

From elegant main dishes to

versatile make-ahead appetizers and

luxurious fireside drinks,

you'll find everything you need to

make this festive season

memorable — and fuss-free!

Clockwise from top: Chèvre Bites with Branston (p.22),
cherry tomatoes filled with Creamy Rice Salad (p.25), Spicy Shrimp Salad
Spring Rolls (p.22), Grilled Chicken Ribbons (p.24).

SPICY SHRIMP SALAD SPRING ROLLS

Elegant and utterly delicious, these appealing make-ahead appetizers (photo, p.21) will be the hit of any festive party or open house — especially since they contain only one gram of fat per roll!

Cut cucumber crosswise into 3 equal lengths. With grater, shred each piece on all sides just down to soft core; discard core. Drain in sieve for 10 minutes.

• In bowl, combine cucumber, carrot and green onions. In small bowl, stir mint sauce into chili sauce; stir in sesame oil. Pour over cucumber mixture and toss gently to combine; let stand for 5 minutes. Drain, reserving dressing.

• Fill another bowl with warm water. Working with 3 rice paper wrappers at a time, soften each by dipping 1 at a time into warm water for about 35 seconds. Lay out in single layer on clean damp tea towel.

• Place 1 tbsp (15 mL) cucumber mixture at top right edge of each rice paper wrapper. Place 1 shrimp on top; fold up bottom edge to cover mixture. Roll up from right to left.

• Repeat with remaining wrappers and filling. *(Rolls can be covered with damp tea towel and refrigerated for up to 6 hours.)* Serve with reserved dressing as dipping sauce. Makes 18 spring rolls.

PER SPRING ROLL: 49 CALORIES, 2 G PROTEIN, 1 G FAT, 8 G CARBOHYDRATE

1	ENGLISH CUCUMBER	1
1-1/2 CUPS	SHREDDED CARROT	375 ML
2	GREEN ONIONS, CHOPPED	2
1/2 CUP	CROSSE & BLACKWELL OLD COUNTRY MINT SAUCE	125 ML
1 TBSP	MAGGI CHILI GARLIC SAUCE	15 ML
1 TSP	SESAME OIL	5 ML
18	ROUND (6-INCH/15 CM) RICE PAPER WRAPPERS	18
18	MEDIUM SHRIMP, COOKED, PEELED AND DEVEINED	18

TIPS: *For a neater look, use a mandoline to shred the carrot and cucumber.*

• For a quick last-minute starter, omit the rice paper and serve the salad mixture and shrimp in small Boston or Bibb lettuce cups.

CHÈVRE BITES WITH BRANSTON

No one will ever guess that anything this tasty and elegant could also be this effortless (photo, p.21)! For a change of flavor, substitute chopped Crosse & Blackwell Mango Chutney or sweet pepper jelly for the Branston.

In food processor, combine chèvre and cream cheese; process with on/off motion until creamy and smooth. Transfer to piping bag fitted with large star tip; pipe into croustades.

• Place on baking sheet; bake in 375°F (190°C) oven for 10 minutes or until cheese peaks turn golden. Garnish each with dab of pickle. Serve immediately. Makes 23 hors d'oeuvres.

PER HORS D'OEUVRE: 52 CALORIES, 2 G PROTEIN, 4 G FAT, 2 G CARBOHYDRATE

TIP: *Mini croustades are available in deli sections of some grocery and specialty food stores — or simply use crackers instead.*

1	PKG (4 OZ/140 G) CHÈVRE (GOAT CHEESE)	1
1	PKG (125 G) CREAM CHEESE	1
23	MINI CROUSTADES (BAKED PASTRY CUPS)	23
2 TBSP	CROSSE & BLACKWELL BRANSTON PICKLE	25 ML

SALMON APPETIZER MOUSSE

Satisfying without being filling, this savory mousse is a perfect start to a festive dinner party.
Make both mousse and herbed mayonnaise ahead, then slice and garnish just before serving.

1	CAN (15.5 OZ/439 G) SALMON	1
1	CAN (385 ML) CARNATION 2% EVAPORATED MILK	1
2	ENVELOPES UNFLAVORED GELATIN	2
1/2 CUP	MAYONNAISE	125 ML
1/3 CUP	LEMON JUICE	75 ML
1/3 CUP	SLICED GREEN ONION	75 ML
1/4 CUP	PARSLEY SPRIGS	50 ML
	SALT AND PEPPER	
	HERBED MAYONNAISE (RECIPE FOLLOWS)	

HERBED MAYONNAISE

1 CUP	PLAIN YOGURT	250 ML
1/2 CUP	MAYONNAISE	125 ML
1/4 CUP	PARSLEY SPRIGS	50 ML
3 TBSP	SLICED GREEN ONION	45 ML
1 TSP	DRIED DILLWEED	5 ML
1/4 TSP	GRANULATED SUGAR	1 ML
	SALT AND PEPPER	

PER SERVING
(WITH MAYONNAISE):
361 CALORIES,
17 G PROTEIN, 29 G FAT,
8 G CARBOHYDRATE,
GOOD SOURCE
OF CALCIUM

Drain salmon, reserving 1/3 cup (75 mL) liquid in saucepan. Break up salmon and discard skin. Set salmon aside.

• Add evaporated milk to salmon liquid. Sprinkle with gelatin; let stand for 10 minutes to soften. Cook, stirring, over low heat until gelatin is dissolved; let cool.

• In food processor, combine gelatin mixture, salmon, mayonnaise, lemon juice, onion and parsley; process until smooth. Add salt and pepper to taste. Pour into 8-1/2- x 4-1/2-inch (1.5 L) loaf pan. Chill for 4 hours or until set. Unmold, slice and serve with Herbed Mayonnaise. Makes 8 servings.

HERBED MAYONNAISE

In food processor, combine yogurt, mayonnaise, parsley, green onion, dill and sugar; process until smooth. Add salt and pepper to taste. Makes about 1-3/4 cups (425 mL).

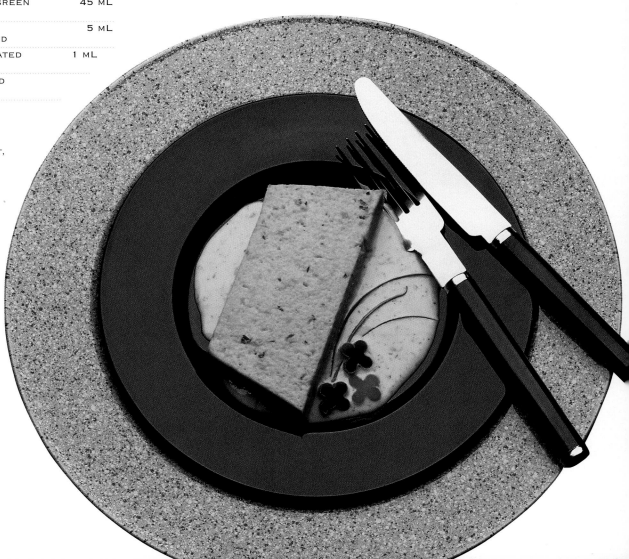

BAKED BRIE WITH CRANBERRY CHUTNEY

Fabulous, festive and ready in just 15 minutes — this is definitely a winner of a holiday recipe!
Our tasty baked Brie also does double duty as a much-appreciated hostess gift or
contribution to a potluck Christmas party.

In small bowl, combine cranberry sauce, chutney, and jalapeño (if using).

• Place Brie round on foil- or parchment paper-lined baking sheet. Spoon cranberry mixture on top. Bake in 350°F (180°C) oven for 10 to 15 minutes or until cheese is starting to melt. With lifter, transfer to serving plate.

• Sprinkle with almonds (if using). Serve with crackers or baguette slices. Makes 6 servings.

PER SERVING: 139 CALORIES, 4 G PROTEIN, 7 G FAT, 15 G CARBOHYDRATE

1/4 CUP	CRANBERRY SAUCE	50 ML
1/4 CUP	CROSSE & BLACKWELL MANGO CHUTNEY	50 ML
1	SMALL JALAPEÑO PEPPER, SEEDED AND FINELY DICED (OPTIONAL)	1
1	BRIE OR CAMEMBERT ROUND (4-INCH/10 CM)	1
1/4 CUP	SLIVERED ALMONDS, TOASTED (OPTIONAL)	50 ML
	CRACKERS OR THIN SLICES OF BAGUETTE	

GRILLED CHICKEN RIBBONS

Chicken is always a crowd-pleaser, especially during the holiday season.
These easy appetizers (photo, p.21) can be made ahead, then grilled at the last minute. For an eye-catching dip,
use honey mustard that's chockful of crunchy mustard seeds.

In small bowl, whisk together mint sauce, olive oil, salt, oregano, paprika, pepper and garlic; transfer to large zipper-type plastic bag.

• Cut chicken into twenty 3- x 1-inch (8 x 2.5 cm) strips. Thread each strip onto soaked 8-inch (20 cm) wooden skewer. Add to marinade in bag; seal and marinate in refrigerator for at least 1 hour or for up to 12 hours.

• Place skewers on greased grill over medium-high heat, keeping exposed end of skewers off hot grill. Cook, turning once, for 10 to 15 minutes or until chicken is no longer pink inside. Serve with Creamy Mustard Sauce for dipping. Makes 20 hors d'oeuvres.

PER HORS D'OEUVRE (WITH DIPPING SAUCE): 59 CALORIES, 5 G PROTEIN, 3 G FAT, 3 G CARBOHYDRATE

1/2 CUP	CROSSE & BLACKWELL MINT SAUCE	125 ML
1/4 CUP	OLIVE OIL	50 ML
1/2 TSP	EACH SALT, CRUSHED DRIED OREGANO AND PAPRIKA	2 ML
1/4 TSP	PEPPER	1 ML
1	CLOVE GARLIC, CRUSHED	1
1 LB	BONELESS SKINLESS CHICKEN BREASTS	500 G
	CREAMY MUSTARD DIPPING SAUCE (RECIPE FOLLOWS)	

CREAMY MUSTARD DIPPING SAUCE

In small bowl, combine 2 tbsp (25 mL) each Crosse & Blackwell Mint Sauce and honey mustard. Stir into 1/4 cup (50 mL) light sour cream. Makes 1/2 cup (125 mL).

TIP: *Chicken Ribbons are just as tasty baked in the oven. Bake in single layer on foil-lined baking sheet in 350°F (180°C) oven for 10 to 15 minutes or until chicken is no longer pink inside.*

CREAMY RICE SALAD

Delight guests with a colorful combo of rice and crunchy vegetables in a creamy lower-fat dressing. Serve this versatile salad as a side dish — or spoon it into endive leaves or hollowed-out cherry tomatoes (see photo, p.21) for a pretty appetizer.

1	PKG (170 G) LONG-GRAIN WHITE AND WILD RICE MIX	1
1 TBSP	POWDERED CHICKEN BOUILLON MIX	15 ML
1 CUP	FINELY DICED SWEET RED OR GREEN PEPPER	250 ML
1/2 CUP	SHREDDED CARROT	125 ML
1/3 CUP	THINLY SLICED GREEN ONION	75 ML
3 TBSP	VINEGAR	45 ML
3/4 CUP	CARNATION 2% EVAPORATED MILK	175 ML
1/2 CUP	LIGHT MAYONNAISE	125 ML
1/4 TSP	PEPPER	1 ML
10 TO 15	CHERRY TOMATOES, HALVED	10 TO 15

Prepare rice mix according to package directions, omitting butter. Stir in chicken bouillon mix; let cool. Add red pepper, carrot and green onion; toss lightly to combine.

• Stir vinegar into evaporated milk until slightly thickened. In bowl, gradually combine with mayonnaise, blending until smooth; stir in pepper. Pour over rice mixture; stir until well coated. Refrigerate for at least 1 hour or for up to 4 hours.

• Transfer to 4-cup (1 L) serving bowl; garnish edge with cherry tomatoes. Makes 6 servings.

PER SERVING: 245 CALORIES, 7 G PROTEIN, 9 G FAT, 34 G CARBOHYDRATE

TIPS: *Be sure the cooked rice mixture has absorbed all water before continuing with recipe. Drain well, if necessary.*

• *For a satisfying main-course salad, add chunked canned tuna or grilled chicken to the cooked rice mixture. Spoon each serving into sectioned tomato (photo, above).*

INDIVIDUAL SEAFOOD QUICHES

*When unexpected holiday guests drop in, these savory mini quiches can be
waiting in the refrigerator or freezer. Ready-made pastry shells and a quick-to-make filling add
to the appeal of this indispensable entertaining recipe.*

In bowl, combine Swiss cheese, salmon, onion, celery, parsley and flour; toss well.

• Place tart shells on baking sheets. Evenly spoon cheese mixture into each.

• In bowl, beat eggs well; beat in evaporated milk and salt. Evenly pour over filling; sprinkle each with 1/4 tsp (1 mL) Parmesan cheese. Bake in 350°F (180°C) oven for 25 minutes or until filling is set. Makes 24 small tarts.

PER TART: 128 CALORIES, 6 G PROTEIN, 8 G FAT, 8 G CARBOHYDRATE

1-1/2 CUPS	FINELY SHREDDED SWISS CHEESE	375 ML
1 CUP	COOKED FLAKED SALMON, TUNA OR SHRIMP	250 ML
1 TBSP	EACH FINELY CHOPPED ONION, CELERY AND FRESH PARSLEY	15 ML
1 TBSP	ALL-PURPOSE FLOUR	15 ML
24	FROZEN OR HOMEMADE 3-INCH (8 CM) TART SHELLS	24
3	EGGS	3
1 CUP	CARNATION 2% EVAPORATED MILK	250 ML
1/4 TSP	SALT	1 ML
2 TBSP	FRESHLY GRATED PARMESAN CHEESE	25 ML

CREAMY MUSHROOM APPETIZERS

*This is carefree holiday entertaining at its best! To save time,
prepare the toast cups and flavorful filling early in the day — then assemble and heat at the last minute.*

In saucepan, melt butter over medium heat; cook mushrooms and green onion, stirring occasionally, until tender and any liquid has evaporated. Blend in flour and salt. Gradually stir in evaporated milk; cook, stirring, until boiling and thickened. Remove from heat.

• Stir in parsley and lemon juice. *(Mixture can be transferred to bowl, covered and refrigerated for up to 8 hours.)* Evenly spoon into Toast Cups; bake in muffin cups in 350°F (180°C) oven for 15 to 20 minutes or until heated through. Makes 48 appetizers.

PER APPETIZER: 91 CALORIES, 3 G PROTEIN, 3 G FAT, 13 G CARBOHYDRATE

1/4 CUP	BUTTER	50 ML
2-1/2 CUPS	FINELY CHOPPED MUSHROOMS	625 ML
1/4 CUP	FINELY CHOPPED GREEN ONION	50 ML
2 TBSP	ALL-PURPOSE FLOUR	25 ML
1/2 TSP	SALT	2 ML
1 CUP	CARNATION 2% EVAPORATED MILK	250 ML
2 TBSP	FINELY CHOPPED FRESH PARSLEY	25 ML
1/2 TSP	LEMON JUICE	2 ML
	TOAST CUPS (SEE BOX, BELOW)	

TOAST CUPS

These quick-to-make toast cups are ideal for a variety of fillings.
• Slightly flatten 48 bread slices. Using 3-inch (8 cm) round cookie cutter, cut 1 round from each bread slice. Press into forty-eight 2-inch (5 cm) greased muffin cups; brush lightly with 1/4 cup (50 mL) melted butter. Bake in 400°F (200°C) oven for 12 minutes or until lightly browned. Let cool. Makes 48 toast cups.

ALFREDO NATASHA FOR TWO

When there's no time to start from scratch, a touch of smoked salmon and the
irresistible flavor of fresh dill transform a convenient frozen entrée into an extraordinary appetizer for two.
For an elegant main-course pasta, simply double the recipe.

1	PKG (275 G) STOUFFER'S FETTUCCINE ALFREDO	1
2 TBSP	SLIVERED SMOKED SALMON	25 mL
1/2 TSP	GRATED LEMON RIND	2 mL
2 TSP	LEMON JUICE	10 mL
1 TSP	CHOPPED FRESH DILL	5 mL

Heat fettuccine Alfredo according to package directions.

• In warmed bowl, combine sauce, pasta, smoked salmon, lemon rind, lemon juice and dill; toss gently. Makes 2 appetizer-size servings.

PER SERVING: 287 CALORIES, 8 G PROTEIN, 19 G FAT, 21 G CARBOHYDRATE

SHRIMP AND GARLIC FETTUCCINE ALFREDO

Extravagant in flavor but not in fat, this deliciously light pasta dish will draw raves from dinner guests every time you serve it. We've included a classic version, too, plus a tasty new take that's spicy with slivered Genoa salami — perfect for a relaxed evening with friends.

In large pot of boiling salted water, cook fettuccine for 8 to 10 minutes or until tender but firm; drain well and return to pot.

• In nonstick skillet, heat oil over medium-high heat; cook garlic and red pepper for 30 seconds or until softened slightly. Add to drained pasta along with evaporated milk and Parmesan cheese. Cook over medium-high heat, stirring gently, for 3 to 4 minutes or until sauce is heated through and thickened slightly.

• Add shrimp and peas; stir gently until heated through. Remove from heat; let stand for 2 to 3 minutes or until thickened. Season with salt and pepper to taste. Garnish each serving with parsley and additional Parmesan cheese, if desired. Makes 4 servings.

PER SERVING: 508 CALORIES, 34 G PROTEIN, 12 G FAT, 66 G CARBOHYDRATE, EXCELLENT SOURCE OF CALCIUM

12 OZ	FETTUCCINE	375 G
1 TSP	OLIVE OIL	5 ML
2	CLOVES GARLIC, MINCED	2
1/2 CUP	DICED SWEET RED PEPPER	125 ML
1	CAN (385 ML) CARNATION 2% EVAPORATED MILK	1
3/4 CUP	(APPROX) FRESHLY GRATED PARMESAN CHEESE	175 ML
5 OZ	MEDIUM SHRIMP, COOKED, PEELED AND DEVEINED	150 G
1/2 CUP	FROZEN PEAS, THAWED	125 ML
	SALT AND PEPPER	
	CHOPPED FRESH PARSLEY (OPTIONAL)	

VARIATIONS

• CLASSIC FETTUCCINE ALFREDO: Omit shrimp, red pepper and peas. After sauce has thickened, stir in 1/4 cup (50 mL) chopped fresh parsley and season with pinch each of ground nutmeg, salt and pepper.

• ALFREDO À LA GENOVESE: Substitute 1 cup (250 mL) slivered Genoa salami or ham for the shrimp.

CREAMY MUSHROOM RISOTTO

Risotto is all the rage — and no wonder. Smooth, creamy and laced with the
wonderful flavor of mushrooms, this is definitely a dish everyone will want to sink a fork into.
For the perfect creamy texture, be sure to use Arborio or other Italian rice.

1-1/2 TSP	OLIVE OIL	7 ML
1	ONION, CHOPPED	1
2	CLOVES GARLIC, FINELY CHOPPED	2
3 CUPS	SLICED FRESH MUSHROOMS (8 OZ/250 G)	750 ML
1-1/3 CUPS	BEEF BROTH	325 ML
3/4 CUP	ARBORIO OR OTHER ITALIAN RICE	175 ML
3/4 TSP	ITALIAN SEASONING	4 ML
1	CAN (385 ML) CARNATION EVAPORATED SKIM MILK	1
2 TBSP	RED WINE	25 ML
2 TBSP	FRESHLY GRATED PARMESAN CHEESE	25 ML
	SALT AND PEPPER	
	CHOPPED FRESH CHIVES OR PARSLEY	

In heavy nonstick saucepan, heat oil over medium-high heat; cook onion and garlic, stirring occasionally, until softened. Add mushrooms; cook, stirring, until moisture is evaporated.

• Stir in beef broth, rice, Italian seasoning and evaporated milk; cook, stirring, until boiling. Reduce heat to low; cover and cook for 10 minutes, stirring frequently.

• Uncover and cook, stirring frequently, for 5 minutes longer or until thick and porridge-like. Stir in wine and Parmesan cheese. Add salt and pepper to taste. Serve immediately garnished with chives. Makes 6 servings.

PER SERVING: 170 CALORIES, 9 G PROTEIN, 2 G FAT, 29 G CARBOHYDRATE

TIP: *Use a combination of mushrooms, if you like — portobello, shiitake, button or porcini.*

CURRIED CHICKEN

*When the weather outside is frightful, bring the warmth of India to the
dinner table with this flavorful curry. Mild enough for even the most timid tastes,
it's especially delicious over hot rice or couscous.*

In large nonstick skillet, heat oil over medium-high heat; cook chicken,
stirring, until browned all over.

- In small bowl, combine evaporated milk, chutney, mustard and curry
powder; pour into skillet. Cook over medium heat,
stirring, until boiling and thickened slightly.

  - Reduce heat, cover and simmer for 5 minutes or
until chicken is no longer pink inside. Makes
4 servings.

TIP: *To
minimize fat,
substitute non-
stick cooking
spray for
vegetable oil.*

PER SERVING: 234 CALORIES, 31 G PROTEIN, 6 G FAT,
14 G CARBOHYDRATE

1 TSP	VEGETABLE OIL	5 ML
1 LB	BONELESS SKINLESS CHICKEN BREASTS, CUT INTO STRIPS	500 G
2/3 CUP	CARNATION 2% EVAPORATED MILK	150 ML
1/3 CUP	CROSSE & BLACKWELL MANGO CHUTNEY	75 ML
3 TBSP	DIJON MUSTARD	45 ML
1 TSP	CURRY POWDER	5 ML

SPICY THAI CHICKEN

*Salsa is the surprise ingredient in a Thai-and-trendy chicken dish that's bursting with flavor.
Evaporated milk guarantees a creamy smoothness that's much lower in fat than a traditional Thai coconut
cream-based sauce. Serve over hot cooked vermicelli noodles or rice.*

TIP: *For authentic Thai flavors,
serve with wedges of fresh lime and
chopped peanuts.*

In large nonstick skillet,
heat oil over medium-
high heat; cook chicken
and onion, stirring, until
browned all over. Stir in
salsa and peanut butter.

- Combine evaporated
milk and cornstarch;
gradually stir into skillet.
Cook, stirring, over
medium heat until boiling
and thickened. Season
with salt and pepper to
taste. Serve garnished
with cilantro. Makes
4 servings.

PER SERVING: 303 CALORIES,
35 G PROTEIN, 11 G FAT,
16 G CARBOHYDRATE,
GOOD SOURCE OF CALCIUM

1 TSP	VEGETABLE OIL	5 ML
1 LB	BONELESS SKINLESS CHICKEN BREASTS, CUT INTO STRIPS	500 G
1/2 CUP	CHOPPED ONION	125 ML
3/4 CUP	MEDIUM SALSA	175 ML
1/4 CUP	LIGHT PEANUT BUTTER	50 ML
1 CUP	CARNATION 2% EVAPORATED MILK	250 ML
1 TSP	CORNSTARCH	5 ML
	SALT AND PEPPER	
	CHOPPED FRESH CILANTRO OR PARSLEY	

Curried Chicken ➤

ORANGE TRUFFLE HOT CHOCOLATE

This adult hot chocolate is the perfect way to warm up after a day of skiing or skating.

1	ENVELOPE (30 G) CHOCOLATE TRUFFLE NESTLÉ CHOCOLAT ROYAL HOT CHOCOLATE MIX	1
3/4 CUP	VERY HOT (NOT BOILING) WATER	175 ML
1 TBSP	EACH ORANGE LIQUEUR AND AMARETTO LIQUEUR	15 ML
	WHIPPED CREAM (OPTIONAL)	

Place hot chocolate mix in 10-ounce (300 mL) mug. Stir in water and orange and amaretto liqueurs until chocolate mix dissolves. Top with whipped cream (if using). Makes 1 serving.

PER SERVING (WITH 1 TBSP/15 ML WHIPPED CREAM): 341 CALORIES, 2 G PROTEIN, 6 G FAT, 47 G CARBOHYDRATE, 13 G ALCOHOL

TIP: *You can use Carnation Hot Chocolate Mix or Nescafé Instant Mocha Café (used in photo) instead of Nestlé Chocolat Royal Hot Chocolate Mix.*

MICROWAVE IRISH COFFEE CREAM

With this make-ahead microwave version, all you need to do is pour and serve.

1	EGG	1
1/3 CUP	GRANULATED SUGAR	75 ML
1	CAN (385 ML) CARNATION 2% EVAPORATED MILK	1
1 TBSP	NESCAFÉ RICH BLEND INSTANT COFFEE	15 ML
1 TSP	NESTLÉ QUIK INSTANT CHOCOLATE DRINK MIX OR SYRUP	5 ML
1/3 CUP	IRISH WHISKEY	75 ML

In microwaveable bowl, beat egg with sugar; set aside.

• In 4-cup (1 L) microwaveable glass measure, combine evaporated milk, instant coffee and chocolate drink mix. Microwave at High for 3 to 4 minutes or until steamy hot. Gradually whisk milk mixture into egg mixture. Microwave at High for 1 minute or until steamy. Strain through sieve; stir in whiskey.

• Pour into airtight container. Cover and refrigerate until chilled. Serve over ice. Makes ten 2-ounce (50 mL) servings.

PER SERVING: 101 CALORIES, 4 G PROTEIN, 1 G FAT, 12 G CARBOHYDRATE, 4 G ALCOHOL

NESCAFÉ COFFEENOG

This whipped version of traditional eggnog holds a delicious hint of coffee. Use only clean, uncracked eggs.

3	EGGS, SEPARATED	3
3 CUPS	MILK	750 ML
1-1/3 CUPS	GRANULATED SUGAR	325 ML
3/4 CUP	COLD WATER	175 ML
1/2 CUP	COGNAC OR RUM	125 ML
3	SACHETS (1.5 G EACH) NESCAFÉ INSTANT ESPRESSO	3
2 TSP	VANILLA	10 ML
1 CUP	WHIPPING CREAM	250 ML

In large bowl, whisk egg yolks. Whisk in milk, 1 cup (250 mL) of the sugar, water, cognac, instant espresso and vanilla; stir until sugar and espresso dissolve. Refrigerate until chilled.

• In bowl, beat egg whites until soft peaks form; gradually beat in remaining sugar until stiff peaks form. Set aside.

• In deep bowl, beat whipping cream until stiff peaks form. Gently fold into milk mixture along with egg whites. Gently stir before serving. Makes 14 servings.

PER SERVING: 215 CALORIES, 4 G PROTEIN, 8 G FAT, 23 G CARBOHYDRATE, 5 G ALCOHOL

TIP: *You can use 7 tsp (35 mL) Nescafé Rich Blend Instant Coffee with 3/4 cup (175 mL) hot water instead of instant espresso and cold water.*

◄ *Orange Truffle Hot Chocolate*

THE SWEETEST CHRISTMAS EVER

Celebrate the comfort and joy of

the season with our most dazzling

desserts ever — from luscious trifles and

tiramisu for the Christmas feast to

cheesecake delights, a sensational

ice cream terrine and soul-warming

fudgy pudding cake. And the sweetest

news of all? You can make many of

these in less time than it takes to recite

"The Night Before Christmas!"

Frozen Tiramisu for Two (p.36)

FROZEN TIRAMISU FOR TWO

*Finally, a tiramisu made just for the two of you! Prepare it just before serving,
then sit back and savor each deliciously creamy spoonful (photo, p.35).*

Line bottom and side of two 1-cup (250 mL) serving bowls or dessert dishes with ladyfingers.

• In small bowl, combine 1 of the instant espresso sachets, water and 3 tbsp (45 mL) of the liqueur until espresso is dissolved. Brush over ladyfingers. Divide half of the chopped candy bar evenly between bowls.

• In food processor or blender, blend together ice cream, remaining sachet instant espresso and liqueur until smooth. Spoon into prepared bowls. Top evenly with remaining chopped candy bar. Serve immediately, garnished with berries (if using). Makes 2 servings.

PER SERVING: 589 CALORIES, 8 G PROTEIN, 23 G FAT, 77 G CARBOHYDRATE, 6 G ALCOHOL

8 TO 10	SMALL SOFT LADYFINGERS, HALVED	8 TO 10
2	SACHETS (1.5 G EACH) NESCAFÉ INSTANT ESPRESSO	2
1/4 CUP	HOT WATER	50 ML
1/4 CUP	COFFEE LIQUEUR	50 ML
1	NESTLÉ CRUNCH CANDY BAR (44 G), CHOPPED	1
4	SCOOPS VANILLA ICE CREAM, SOFTENED	4
	FRESH BERRIES (OPTIONAL)	

COCOA CRÈME

*Here's a delightfully decadent dessert that's easy to prepare,
has enough chocolate flavor to satisfy even the most fervent chocoholic and is low in fat.
What more could you ask for, especially at Christmas?*

Divide jam among six 3/4-cup (175 mL) custard cups; set aside.

• In large bowl, combine sugar and cocoa; stir in egg yolks and egg until blended and smooth. Gradually whisk in evaporated milk.

• In small bowl, combine water and instant coffee until dissolved; whisk into cocoa mixture. Strain and divide evenly among custard cups.

• Place custard cups in 13- x 9-inch (3.5 L) cake pan. Pour in enough hot water to come three-quarters of the way up sides of cups; cover pan with foil. Bake in 325°F (160°C) oven for 45 to 50 minutes or until knife inserted at edge of custard comes out clean but center is still jiggly.

• Remove cups from pan; let cool on rack to room temperature. Refrigerate for at least 1 hour or until chilled. Makes 6 servings.

PER SERVING: 205 CALORIES, 8 G PROTEIN, 5 G FAT, 32 G CARBOHYDRATE, GOOD SOURCE OF CALCIUM

TIP: *Before serving, top cooked custards with sliced bananas, chopped toasted pecans and a drizzle of Velvety Fudge Sauce (p.39) or Brandy Toffee Sauce (p.38).*

2 TBSP	RASPBERRY JAM, STRAINED	25 ML
1/2 CUP	GRANULATED SUGAR	125 ML
1/2 CUP	SIFTED UNSWEETENED COCOA POWDER	125 ML
2	EGG YOLKS	2
1	EGG	1
1	CAN (385 ML) CARNATION 2% EVAPORATED MILK	1
1/2 CUP	HOT WATER	125 ML
2 TSP	NESCAFÉ RICH BLEND INSTANT COFFEE	10 ML

ESPRESSO–CHIP ICE CREAM TERRINE

Simple but sensational, this dazzling make-ahead dessert is perfect for
holiday entertaining. Top cut slices with fresh berries and a drizzle of Brandy Toffee Sauce (recipe, p.38).

4 CUPS	VANILLA ICE CREAM, SOFTENED	1 L
2	SACHETS (1.5 G EACH) NESCAFÉ INSTANT ESPRESSO	2
8	CHOCOLATE-COVERED ESPRESSO BEANS, CHOPPED (OR 3 TBSP/45 ML CHOPPED SEMISWEET CHOCOLATE)	8
3 TBSP	COARSELY CHOPPED TOASTED ALMONDS (OPTIONAL)	45 ML

Line 8-1/2- x 4-1/2-inch (1.5 L) loaf pan with plastic wrap; chill in freezer.

• Meanwhile, in blender or food processor, blend ice cream with instant espresso until smooth; pour into large bowl. Quickly stir in chopped espresso beans, and almonds (if using). Pour into chilled pan. Freeze for 8 hours or until firm. *(Terrine can be wrapped tightly in plastic wrap and frozen for up to 3 weeks.)*

• To serve, unmold onto cutting board; remove plastic wrap and cut terrine into 1/2-inch (1 cm) thick slices. Makes 12 servings.

PER SERVING: 123 CALORIES, 2 G PROTEIN, 7 G FAT, 13 G CARBOHYDRATE

CAPPUCCINO CHEESECAKES

Surprise your guests with a delicious new twist on two popular dessert companions —
cappuccino and cheesecake. These appealing in-a-cup desserts are ideal for a holiday buffet. We've also included
instructions for a larger flan.

In small bowl, combine graham cracker crumbs, brown sugar and cinnamon; stir in butter until moistened. Divide evenly among 6 cappuccino cups or custard cups, pressing with fingertips or bottom of small glass. Refrigerate until chilled.

• FILLING: Meanwhile, in large bowl, beat cream cheese until fluffy. Beat in eggs, one at a time, beating well after each addition. Beat in sugar, instant espresso, cognac and vanilla. Divide evenly among cups.

• Place cups in 13- x 9-inch (3.5 L) cake pan. Pour in enough hot water to come 1 inch (2.5 cm) up sides of cups. Bake in 375°F (190°C) oven for 15 to 20 minutes or until puffed and center feels set when lightly touched. Remove from water and let stand at room temperature until cooled. Refrigerate for 3 hours or until chilled.

• GARNISH: In deep bowl, beat whipping cream with maple syrup until stiff peaks form. Spoon onto each cheesecake; sprinkle with cinnamon. Makes 6 servings.

PER SERVING: 593 CALORIES, 10 G PROTEIN, 42 G FAT, 42 G CARBOHYDRATE, 1 G ALCOHOL

VARIATION

• CAPPUCCINO CHEESECAKE FLAN: Instead of cappuccino cups, use 8-inch (20 cm) springform pan; bake for 25 to 30 minutes. Makes 8 to 10 servings.

1/2 CUP	GRAHAM CRACKER CRUMBS	125 ML
3 TBSP	PACKED BROWN SUGAR	45 ML
1/4 TSP	GROUND CINNAMON	1 ML
2 TBSP	BUTTER, MELTED	25 ML
	FILLING	
2	PKG (250 G EACH) CREAM CHEESE, SOFTENED	2
2	EGGS	2
1/2 CUP	GRANULATED SUGAR	125 ML
2	SACHETS (1.5 G EACH) NESCAFÉ INSTANT ESPRESSO	2
2 TBSP	COGNAC OR COFFEE LIQUEUR	25 ML
1/2 TSP	VANILLA	2 ML
	GARNISH	
1/2 CUP	WHIPPING CREAM	125 ML
2 TBSP	MAPLE SYRUP	25 ML
	GROUND CINNAMON	

BRANDY TOFFEE SAUCE

When you want a change from chocolate, indulge
in a drizzle of this luxurious sauce over chocolate ice cream or fruit.

Smack wrapped toffee on counter to break bars. Unwrap; place in 2-cup (500 mL) microwaveable glass measure or bowl. Add evaporated milk; microwave at High for 2 minutes, stirring twice.

• Microwave at High for 15 to 30 seconds longer or until bubbling; stir until smooth. Stir in brandy to taste. *(Sauce can be refrigerated for up to 1 week. To serve, bring to room temperature or heat slightly.)* Makes about 1 cup (250 mL), enough for 10 servings.

PER SERVING: 121 CALORIES, 1 G PROTEIN, 5 G FAT, 17 G CARBOHYDRATE, 0.5 G ALCOHOL

4	BARS (56 G EACH) MACKINTOSH'S CREAMY TOFFEE	4
1/3 CUP	CARNATION EVAPORATED MILK	75 ML
1 TO 2 TBSP	BRANDY OR COGNAC	15 TO 25 ML

MOCHA MERINGUE CLOUDS

These light-as-a-cloud desserts are a perfect finish to the Christmas feast. Best of all, the filling and meringues can be made ahead and assembled just before serving.

3	EGG WHITES	3
1 TSP	UNSWEETENED COCOA POWDER, SIFTED	5 ML
1/2 TSP	NESCAFÉ INSTANT ESPRESSO	2 ML
PINCH	EACH SALT AND CREAM OF TARTAR	PINCH
1/3 CUP	GRANULATED SUGAR	75 ML
1 OZ	SEMISWEET CHOCOLATE (1 SQUARE)	30 G
	FILLING	
1 CUP	WHIPPING CREAM	250 ML
1	SACHET (1.5 G) NESCAFÉ INSTANT ESPRESSO	1
3 TBSP	ICING SUGAR	45 ML
1/2 TSP	VANILLA	2 ML
10 TO 12	FRESH STRAWBERRIES, SLICED	10 TO 12

Line 2 baking sheets with parchment or brown paper. Trace nine 3-inch (8 cm) circles on paper. Set aside.

• In large bowl, combine egg whites, cocoa powder, instant espresso, salt and cream of tartar; beat until soft peaks form. Gradually beat in sugar, beating until stiff peaks form. Spoon onto circles, spreading to fill each and forming hollow in centers.

• Bake in 200°F (100°C) oven for 1-1/2 to 2 hours or until just beginning to brown slightly. Turn oven off. Leave meringues in oven with door closed for at least 1 hour or until dry.

TIP: *Use 3-inch (8 cm) round glass as pattern for meringue circles.*

• In small microwaveable cup, heat chocolate on Low for 1 minute or until melted. With fork, drizzle across meringue shells.

• FILLING: In deep bowl, beat together whipping cream, instant espresso, icing sugar and vanilla until stiff peaks form. Spoon into meringue shells just before serving. Arrange strawberry slices on top. Makes 9 servings.

PER SERVING: 158 CALORIES, 2 G PROTEIN, 10 G FAT, 15 G CARBOHYDRATE

VELVETY FUDGE SAUCE

Versatile, ready in just minutes and a dream over ice cream or anything else your heart desires, this luscious dessert sauce also makes a much appreciated hostess gift.

1	PKG (175 G) SEMISWEET CHOCOLATE CHIPS (1 CUP/250 ML)	1
1/2 CUP	CORN SYRUP	125 ML
1 CUP	CARNATION EVAPORATED MILK	250 ML

In small saucepan, cook chocolate chips and corn syrup, stirring, over low heat until chocolate melts and mixture is smooth. Remove from heat.

• Gradually blend in evaporated milk. Serve warm or at room temperature. *(Sauce can be refrigerated in airtight container for up to 1 week. To serve, bring to room temperature or heat slightly.)* Makes about 2 cups (500 mL), enough for 20 servings.

PER SERVING: 96 CALORIES, 1 G PROTEIN, 4 G FAT, 14 G CARBOHYDRATE

TIPS: *For the adventurous, stir in 1 to 2 tbsp (15 to 25 mL) of your favorite liqueur when adding evaporated milk.*

• *For a hostess gift, pour into decorative mason jar.*

BERRY GOOD PARFAITS

Rich in flavor and surprisingly low in fat, these easy-to-make parfaits
(featured on the cover) are an elegant ending to any festive meal. Serve in pretty sorbet or parfait glasses.

In saucepan, bring cranberries, sugar and water to boil; reduce heat and simmer, uncovered and stirring occasionally, for about 5 minutes or until berries have popped.

• In blender, blend together jelly powder and boiling water until dissolved. Add cranberry mixture; blend until smooth. Transfer to large bowl. Chill until almost set.

• Beat jelly mixture until frothy. Gradually beat in chilled evaporated milk; beat until light and airy. Pour into parfait glasses; chill until set. Makes 5 servings.

1-1/2 CUPS	CRANBERRIES (FRESH OR FROZEN)	375 ML
3/4 CUP	GRANULATED SUGAR	175 ML
1/2 CUP	WATER	125 ML
1	PKG (85 G) ORANGE JELLY POWDER	1
1 CUP	BOILING WATER	250 ML
1 CUP	CARNATION 2% EVAPORATED MILK, CHILLED	250 ML

PER SERVING: 229 CALORIES, 4 G PROTEIN, 1 G FAT, 51 G CARBOHYDRATE

CAFÉ AU LAIT CRÈME BRÛLÉE

Coffee and dessert in one delicious spoonful! Although this luscious end-of-dinner
favorite may look complicated to make, you'll be delighted with the ease of preparation — and the results.

In saucepan, combine evaporated milk, water and instant coffee; cook, stirring, over medium heat just until bubbles form around edge of pan. Add granulated sugar, vanilla and salt; stir until sugar is dissolved.

• In large bowl, beat eggs well; gradually stir in hot milk mixture. Strain through fine sieve into six 3/4-cup (175 mL) custard cups.

• Place custard cups in 13- x 9-inch (3.5 L) cake pan. Pour in enough hot water to come halfway up sides of cups. Bake in 300°F (150°C) oven for 25 to 30 minutes or until knife inserted near center comes out clean.

• Remove custard cups from pan; let cool on rack to room temperature. Refrigerate for at least 1 hour or until chilled.

• Just before serving, sieve thin even layer of brown sugar over custards. Place as close as possible under preheated broiler. Watching carefully to avoid burning, broil for 50 to 60 seconds or until sugar is melted. Sieve another layer of brown sugar over top; broil until sugar is melted and browned slightly. Serve immediately. Makes 6 servings.

1	CAN (385 ML) CARNATION EVAPORATED MILK	1
1 CUP	WATER	250 ML
4 TSP	NESCAFÉ RICH BLEND INSTANT COFFEE	20 ML
2/3 CUP	GRANULATED SUGAR	150 ML
1 TSP	VANILLA	5 ML
1/4 TSP	SALT	1 ML
4	EGGS	4
1/4 CUP	(APPROX) PACKED BROWN SUGAR	50 ML

TIP: *Instead of individual custard cups, you can use a 5-cup (1.25 L) shallow baking dish.*

PER SERVING: 261 CALORIES, 9 G PROTEIN, 9 G FAT, 36 G CARBOHYDRATE, GOOD SOURCE OF CALCIUM

CAFÉ ALEXANDER

When the last of the presents has been wrapped, treat yourself and someone special to a few relaxed moments by the fire — and this luscious, decidedly grown-up dessert. For a hit of mocha, use chocolate ice cream instead of vanilla.

In blender or food processor, blend 4 scoops softened vanilla ice cream with 1 sachet (1.5 g) Nescafé Instant Espresso and 1 tbsp (15 mL) cognac until smooth. Spoon into chilled champagne glasses or dessert cups. Makes two 1/2-cup (125 mL) servings.

Per serving: 309 Calories, 5 g Protein, 15 g Fat, 35 g Carbohydrate, 2 g Alcohol, Good Source of Calcium

CHRISTMAS CRANBERRY DESSERT

*An invitation for dessert and coffee is one of the most relaxing ways to
celebrate the holidays with favorite friends and neighbors. With this festive make-ahead dessert,
you'll be able to enjoy the celebrating, too!*

1	PKG (285 G) MINIATURE RASPBERRY JELLY ROLLS	1
1	PKG (170 G) RASPBERRY JELLY POWDER	1
2/3 CUP	GRANULATED SUGAR	150 ML
2 CUPS	BOILING WATER	500 ML
1 CUP	FINELY CHOPPED FRESH CRANBERRIES	250 ML
2/3 CUP	CARNATION INSTANT SKIM MILK POWDER	150 ML
2/3 CUP	ICE WATER	150 ML
2 TBSP	ORANGE JUICE	25 ML

Cut jelly rolls into 1/4-inch (5 mm) thick slices.
Cover bottom of 9-inch (23 cm) springform pan
with some of the slices; stand remaining slices
around edge of pan.

• In large bowl, dissolve jelly powder and sugar
in boiling water; add cranberries. Chill until
mixture mounds when lifted on spoon.

• Meanwhile, in small bowl, beat skim milk
powder and ice water at high speed for 3 to
4 minutes or until soft peaks form. Add orange
juice. Beat for 3 to 4 minutes or until stiff
peaks form.

• Fold whipped milk into cranberry mixture. Pour into prepared pan.
Chill for 1 to 3 hours or until set. Makes 8 servings.

PER SERVING: 283 CALORIES, 6 G PROTEIN, 3 G FAT, 58 G CARBOHYDRATE

TIP: *Instead of
miniature
raspberry jelly
rolls, you can
use 1 pkg (298 g)
frozen pound
cake, thawed
and cut into
1/4-inch (5 mm)
thick slices.*

LIGHT CRANBERRY-ORANGE TRIFLE

*One spoonful of this lightened-up holiday classic will prove that desserts don't have to be high in fat
to taste fabulous. The secret is in the creamy custard, made with 2% evaporated milk instead of higher-fat cream
— but no one will ever guess!*

1/2 CUP	GRANULATED SUGAR	125 ML
3 TBSP	CORNSTARCH	45 ML
1	CAN (385 ML) CARNATION 2% EVAPORATED MILK	1
1 CUP	WATER	250 ML
2	EGGS, BEATEN	2
1 TSP	EACH VANILLA AND GRATED ORANGE RIND	5 ML
1	ANGEL FOOD CAKE (400 G), CUBED	1
1/4 CUP	ORANGE JUICE	50 ML
1	CAN (398 ML) WHOLE-BERRY CRANBERRY SAUCE, STIRRED	1

In saucepan, combine sugar and cornstarch. Gradually stir in
evaporated milk and water; cook, stirring, over medium heat until
boiling and thickened. Reduce heat; cook for 1 minute longer.

• Whisk small amount of hot milk mixture into eggs; stir egg mixture
back into saucepan. Cook, stirring, until thickened. Remove from heat.
Add vanilla and orange rind. Place plastic wrap directly on surface;
refrigerate for about 2 hours or until chilled.

• Arrange half of the cake cubes over bottom of 8-cup (2 L) glass bowl;
sprinkle with half of the orange juice. Top with half of the cranberry
sauce, then half of the custard. Repeat layers once. Cover and refrigerate
for at least 2 hours or for up to 12 hours. Makes 8 servings.

PER SERVING: 351 CALORIES, 8 G PROTEIN, 3 G FAT, 73 G CARBOHYDRATE,
GOOD SOURCE OF CALCIUM

◄ *Christmas Cranberry Dessert*

MINCEMEAT STREUSEL BREAD PUDDING

What could be better after a day of skiing, skating or tobogganing than this satisfying bread pudding with a festive twist. Add a dollop of creamy custard sauce (recipe follows) and you have heaven on a spoon!

Arrange half of the bread cubes in greased 9-inch (23 cm) deep-dish pie plate or fluted quiche dish. Spoon mincemeat over top. Cover with remaining bread cubes. In bowl, beat together eggs, evaporated milk, vanilla and cinnamon; pour evenly over bread cubes. Let stand for 10 minutes.

• In separate bowl, combine flour and brown sugar; with pastry blender or two knives, cut in butter until mixture resembles coarse crumbs. Sprinkle over bread cube mixture. Bake in 350°F (180°C) oven for 30 to 35 minutes or until knife inserted in center comes out clean. Let stand for 10 minutes before serving with Jiffy Custard Sauce. Makes 8 servings.

PER SERVING (WITH SAUCE): 388 CALORIES, 10 G PROTEIN, 11 G FAT, 75 G CARBOHYDRATE, GOOD SOURCE OF CALCIUM

JIFFY CUSTARD SAUCE

In saucepan, combine 2 tbsp (25 mL) each vanilla custard powder and granulated sugar. Gradually stir in 2/3 cup (150 mL) Carnation 2% Evaporated Milk and 1/2 cup (125 mL) water; cook, stirring, over medium heat until boiling and thickened. Serve warm or cool. Makes about 1-1/4 cups (300 mL).

5 CUPS	CUBED (1/2-INCH/1 CM) DAY-OLD FRENCH BREAD	1.25 L
1-1/2 CUPS	PREPARED MINCEMEAT	375 ML
3	EGGS	3
1	CAN (385 ML) CARNATION 2% EVAPORATED MILK	1
1 TSP	VANILLA	5 ML
3/4 TSP	GROUND CINNAMON	4 ML
1/2 CUP	ALL-PURPOSE FLOUR	125 ML
1/2 CUP	PACKED BROWN SUGAR	125 ML
1/4 CUP	BUTTER	50 ML
	JIFFY CUSTARD SAUCE (RECIPE FOLLOWS)	

FUDGY PUDDING CAKE

Deliciously chocolaty and delightfully light, this is one dessert you'll want to make often.
Serve hot from the oven and top with vanilla ice cream or cappuccino gelato.

3/4 CUP	BOILING WATER	175 ML
2 TSP	NESCAFÉ RICH BLEND INSTANT COFFEE	10 ML
3/4 CUP	CARNATION EVAPORATED SKIM MILK	175 ML
1 CUP	ALL-PURPOSE FLOUR	250 ML
1/2 CUP	GRANULATED SUGAR	125 ML
1/3 CUP	SIFTED UNSWEETENED COCOA POWDER	75 ML
1 TBSP	BAKING POWDER	15 ML
1/4 TSP	SALT	1 ML
2 TBSP	BUTTER, MELTED	25 ML
	FUDGY SAUCE	
1/4 CUP	GRANULATED SUGAR	50 ML
2 TBSP	SIFTED UNSWEETENED COCOA POWDER	25 ML

In 2-cup (500 mL) measuring cup, combine boiling water and instant coffee until coffee is dissolved. Stir in evaporated milk; set aside.

• In bowl, combine flour, sugar, cocoa, baking powder and salt; stir in butter and half of the coffee mixture until smooth (batter will be thick). Spoon into lightly greased 8-cup (2 L) round ovenproof bowl or casserole, smoothing top.

• FUDGY SAUCE: In small bowl, combine sugar and cocoa; sprinkle over batter. Pour remaining coffee mixture over top. Do not stir.

• Bake in 350°F (180°C) oven for 35 minutes or until sauce bubbles and cake is firm to the touch. Serve hot. Makes 8 servings.

PER SERVING: 196 CALORIES, 4 G PROTEIN, 4 G FAT, 36 G CARBOHYDRATE

VARIATION

• SPIRITED FUDGY PUDDING CAKE: Add 2 tbsp (25 mL) dark rum to dissolved instant coffee.

APPLE ALMOND CRISP

Serve this crisp warm for dessert, cut into large squares and topped with vanilla ice cream — or let it cool
and cut into bars for snacking with hot chocolate or mulled cider after a winter's day outdoors.

1-1/2 CUPS	ALL-PURPOSE FLOUR	375 ML
1/2 CUP	ROLLED OATS	125 ML
1/4 CUP	PACKED BROWN SUGAR	50 ML
1/2 TSP	GROUND CINNAMON	2 ML
3/4 CUP	BUTTER, SOFTENED	175 ML
3	APPLES, PEELED, HALVED, CORED AND CUT INTO THIN SLICES	3
4	BARS (56 G EACH) MACKINTOSH'S CREAMY TOFFEE	4
1/3 CUP	CARNATION EVAPORATED MILK	75 ML
1/2 CUP	SLICED ALMONDS	125 ML

In large bowl, combine flour, rolled oats, sugar and cinnamon. With pastry blender or 2 knives, cut in butter until mixture resembles coarse crumbs. Remove 1/3 cup (75 mL) crumb mixture and set aside.

• Press remaining mixture onto bottom of lightly greased 13- x 9-inch (3.5 L) cake pan. Arrange apple slices in single layer of overlapping rows to cover base. Set aside.

• Smack wrapped toffee on counter to break bars. Unwrap; place in 2-cup (500 mL) microwaveable glass measure or bowl. Add evaporated milk; microwave at High for 2 minutes, stirring twice. Microwave at High for 15 to 30 seconds longer or until bubbling; stir until smooth. Drizzle evenly over apples. Add almonds to reserved crumb mixture; sprinkle evenly over top.

• Bake in 375°F (190°C) oven for 40 to 45 minutes or until apples are softened and caramel mixture begins to bubble. Let cool slightly before slicing to serve. Makes 12 servings.

PER SERVING: 330 CALORIES, 4 G PROTEIN, 18 G FAT, 38 G CARBOHYDRATE

LUSCIOUS TURTLES CHEESECAKE

If you like Turtles, you'll love this irresistible new way to indulge — bite after creamy-smooth,
chocolate-and-caramel bite. If you dare, top with Brandy Toffee Sauce (recipe, p.38).

In bowl, combine graham cracker crumbs, pecans, butter and granulated sugar, mixing well. Press onto bottom and up side of 9-inch (23 cm) springform pan. Bake in 325°F (160°C) oven for 12 minutes; refrigerate until chilled.

• In large bowl, beat cream cheese until smooth; beat in brown sugar, flour and vanilla until well blended. Add eggs, one at a time, beating well after each addition. Stir in chopped candies; pour into graham crust. Bake in 325°F (160°C) oven for 50 to 60 minutes or until center is just set.

• Turn oven off; let cake stand in warm oven with door closed for 1-1/2 hours. Let cool to room temperature on wire rack. Remove side of pan; refrigerate until chilled before serving. Makes 10 servings.

Per serving: 565 Calories, 11 g Protein, 37 g Fat, 47 g Carbohydrate

1-1/4 CUPS	GRAHAM CRACKER CRUMBS	300 ML
1/2 CUP	FINELY CHOPPED PECANS	125 ML
1/4 CUP	BUTTER, MELTED	50 ML
2 TBSP	GRANULATED SUGAR	25 ML
3	PKG (250 G EACH) CREAM CHEESE, SOFTENED	3
3/4 CUP	PACKED BROWN SUGAR	175 ML
1 TBSP	ALL-PURPOSE FLOUR	15 ML
2 TSP	VANILLA	10 ML
3	EGGS	3
14	TURTLES CANDIES, CHOPPED	14

CHERRY POUND CAKE

This delectable freezer-friendly cake is an easier alternative to traditional fruitcake. For a change of taste, try the
chocolate-chip variation — or bake up both, and get a head start on holiday entertaining!

Grease and flour 12-cup (3 L) bundt or tube pan; set aside.

• In large bowl, beat together sugar, butter, eggs and almond extract at low speed until blended; beat at high speed for about 5 minutes or until light and fluffy.

• Stir together flour, baking powder and salt; add to creamed mixture alternately with evaporated milk, making three additions of dry mixture and two of evaporated milk. Fold in cherries.

• Turn batter into prepared pan. Bake in 350°F (180°C) oven for 55 minutes; cover loosely with foil and bake for 15 to 20 minutes longer or until cake tester inserted in center comes out clean. Let cool in pan on rack for 10 minutes. Remove from pan; let cool completely. Dust with icing sugar. Makes 16 slices.

Per slice: 422 Calories, 6 g Protein, 18 g Fat, 59 g Carbohydrate

2-3/4 CUPS	GRANULATED SUGAR	675 ML
1-1/4 CUPS	BUTTER, SOFTENED	300 ML
5	EGGS	5
1 TSP	ALMOND EXTRACT	5 ML
3 CUPS	ALL-PURPOSE FLOUR	750 ML
1 TSP	BAKING POWDER	5 ML
1/4 TSP	SALT	1 ML
1 CUP	CARNATION EVAPORATED MILK	250 ML
2 CUPS	QUARTERED MARASCHINO CHERRIES, WELL DRAINED	500 ML
	SIFTED ICING SUGAR	

VARIATION

• CHOCOLATY CHIP POUND CAKE: Omit almond extract. Use miniature chocolate chips instead of cherries.

CROWD-PLEASING CARAMEL CORN

When winter entertaining switches from elegant to extra-easy, gather the gang for an evening of videos and a big bowlful of caramel corn. In fact, why not surprise all the film buffs on your gift list with a video — and their own supply of this irresistible treat?

• Prepare 1 pkg (100 g) plain or light microwave popcorn according to package directions. Empty into large microwaveable glass bowl; discard unpopped kernels.

• Smack 3 wrapped bars (56 g each) Mackintosh's Creamy Toffee on counter to break bars. Unwrap; place in 2-cup (500 mL) microwaveable glass measure or bowl. Add 3 tbsp (45 mL) butter and 1 tbsp (15 mL) milk; microwave at High, stirring once, for 2 to 2-1/2 minutes or until boiling.

• Stir caramel mixture; pour over popcorn, stirring until coated.

Microwave at High for 2 to 3 minutes or until heated through (bowl will be hot). Pour out onto foil-lined baking sheet. Let cool for 10 to 15 minutes or until crisp. Makes eight 1-cup (250 mL) servings.

PER SERVING: 185 CALORIES, 2 G PROTEIN, 9 G FAT, 24 G CARBOHYDRATE

TIP: *If caramel corn is still sticky after cooling, microwave for an additional 1 to 1-1/2 minutes.*

TOFFEE APPLE CAKE

Special enough for company, easy enough for kids to help bake, this moist and chewy toffee-soaked cake is a perfect dessert for the relaxing side of Christmas. Just make sure you have enough on hand for seconds!

2-1/2 CUPS	ALL-PURPOSE FLOUR	625 ML
2 CUPS	GRANULATED SUGAR	500 ML
2 TSP	SALT	10 ML
1-1/2 TSP	BAKING SODA	7 ML
1/2 TSP	BAKING POWDER	2 ML
2 CUPS	CHOPPED PEELED APPLES	500 ML
1-1/4 CUPS	CARNATION EVAPORATED MILK	300 ML
1/3 CUP	WATER	75 ML
2	EGGS, LIGHTLY BEATEN	2
1/3 CUP	PACKED BROWN SUGAR	75 ML
1 CUP	FLAKED COCONUT	250 ML
1/2 CUP	CHOPPED PECANS	125 ML
3	BARS (56 G EACH) MACKINTOSH'S CREAMY TOFFEE	3

In large bowl, combine flour, sugar, salt, baking soda and baking powder.

• In separate bowl, combine apples, 1/2 cup (125 mL) of the evaporated milk, water and eggs; stir into dry ingredients to mix well.

• Spread in greased 13- x 9-inch (3.5 L) cake pan. Sprinkle brown sugar, then coconut and pecans over top. Bake in 350°F (180°C) oven for 45 to 50 minutes or until center springs back when lightly touched, covering loosely with foil if topping browns too quickly.

• Smack wrapped toffee on counter to break bars. Unwrap; place in 4-cup (1 L) microwaveable glass measure or bowl along with remaining evaporated milk. Microwave at High for 5 minutes, stirring twice, or until smooth. Pour evenly over hot cake. Let cool completely before serving. Makes 12 servings.

PER SERVING: 451 CALORIES, 6 G PROTEIN, 11 G FAT, 82 G CARBOHYDRATE

FAMILY ON THE RUN

When the hectic pace

of getting ready for the

holidays leaves little

time for preparing family

meals, dip into our culinary

survival kit. You'll find

nourishing dishes that taste

great, are ready in minutes

— and are guaranteed to

recharge you for the festive

activities ahead.

Microwave Minestrone in Minutes (p.50)

MICROWAVE MINESTRONE IN MINUTES

This satisfying homestyle soup for two (photo, p.49) is ready in the time it takes to heat up a convenient frozen entrée.
If you hide the pack, no one will ever guess how easy it was to make!

Microwave spaghetti and sauce at High for 3 minutes according to package directions. Cut pasta into bite-size pieces; transfer to 4-cup (1 L) microwaveable glass measure or bowl.

• Stir in chicken broth, beans and Swiss chard. Cover loosely; microwave at High for 6 minutes or until steaming. Ladle into warmed bowls; sprinkle with Parmesan cheese (if using). Makes 2 servings.

PER SERVING: 318 CALORIES, 19 G PROTEIN, 6 G FAT, 47 G CARBOHYDRATE, VERY HIGH IN FIBER

1	PKG (320 G) STOUFFER'S LEAN CUISINE SPAGHETTI	1
1-1/2 CUPS	CHICKEN BROTH	375 ML
1 CUP	LIBBY'S CHILI STYLE RED KIDNEY BEANS	250 ML
1/3 CUP	SHREDDED SWISS CHARD OR SPINACH LEAVES	75 ML
	FRESHLY GRATED PARMESAN CHEESE (OPTIONAL)	

JUST-FOR-KIDS SOUP

Thank goodness for soups with a sense of humor! Serve up a bowlful of this fun soup
the next time your little ones descend on the kitchen demanding something quick and delicious.
While the soup heats up, let them cut out toast shapes with cookie cutters to eat alongside.

In 4-cup (1 L) microwaveable glass measure or bowl, combine spaghetti sauce, water, pasta and sauce, beans, and chili powder (if using).

• Cover loosely; microwave at High for 4 to 5 minutes or until steaming. Serve sprinkled with Parmesan cheese (if using). Makes 4 servings.

PER SERVING: 222 CALORIES, 8 G PROTEIN, 6 G FAT, 34 G CARBOHYDRATE, VERY HIGH IN FIBER

1 CUP	SPAGHETTI SAUCE	250 ML
1 CUP	WATER	250 ML
1	CAN (14 OZ/398 ML) LIBBY'S ALPHA-GETTI, ZOODLES OR DINO-GETTI PASTA AND SAUCE	1
1 CUP	LIBBY'S CHILI STYLE RED KIDNEY BEANS, DRAINED (OR LIBBY'S DEEP-BROWNED BEANS IN TOMATO SAUCE)	250 ML
1 TSP	CHILI POWDER (OPTIONAL)	5 ML
	FRESHLY GRATED PARMESAN CHEESE (OPTIONAL)	

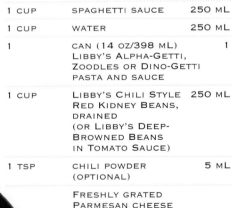

SAUCY PASTA CARBONARA

Presto — pasta! That's almost how quickly you'll have a delicious pasta dinner on the table, when you take advantage of convenient frozen pasta with vegetables, plus the goodness of eggs, milk and cheese.

1	PKG (500 G) FROZEN MIXED PASTA AND VEGETABLES	1
1	CAN (385 ML) CARNATION 2% EVAPORATED MILK	1
1/3 CUP	CUBED LEAN HAM	75 ML
2 TBSP	FRESHLY GRATED PARMESAN CHEESE	25 ML
1/4 TSP	EACH GARLIC POWDER AND CRUSHED DRIED OREGANO	1 ML
1	EGG, LIGHTLY BEATEN	1
	SALT AND PEPPER	
	CHOPPED FRESH PARSLEY	

In heavy saucepan, cook pasta and vegetable mixture according to package directions.

• Stir in evaporated milk, ham, Parmesan cheese, garlic powder and oregano; cook, stirring, over medium-high heat until boiling and thickened slightly. Remove from heat.

• Beat small amount of sauce into egg. Stir egg mixture back into saucepan; heat gently for 30 seconds or until just thickened slightly. Add salt and pepper to taste. Serve garnished with parsley. Makes 2 servings.

TIP: *For a change of taste, substitute chopped cooked bacon, Genoa salami or prosciutto for ham.*

PER SERVING: 488 CALORIES, 39 G PROTEIN, 12 G FAT, 122 G CARBOHYDRATE, EXCELLENT SOURCE OF CALCIUM

PANTRY SEAFOOD CHOWDER

*With a well-stocked pantry (see box, below), satisfying suppers such as this family-pleasing
chowder are both quick to make and easy on the cook — especially during the pre-Christmas rush.
Serve with thick slices of French bread and a toss of greens.*

1	CAN (5 OZ/142 G) CLAMS	1
1 TSP	VEGETABLE OIL	5 ML
1	MEDIUM ONION, CHOPPED	1
1	LARGE POTATO, PEELED AND DICED	1
1	PKG (400 G) FROZEN FISH FILLETS, PARTIALLY THAWED AND CUT INTO BITE-SIZE PIECES	1
1	CAN (10 OZ/284 ML) CREAM-STYLE CORN	1
1	CAN (385 ML) CARNATION LIGHT OR 2% EVAPORATED MILK	1
	SALT AND PEPPER	

Drain clams, reserving liquid; set clams aside. Add enough water to clam liquid to make 1 cup (250 mL); set aside.

• In large heavy saucepan, heat oil over medium-high heat; cook onion, stirring, until softened. Add reserved clam liquid and potato; bring to boil. Reduce heat and simmer for 5 minutes or until potato is just cooked.

• Add fish, corn and evaporated milk; cook, stirring, over medium heat for 6 to 7 minutes or until fish flakes easily when tested with fork. Stir in clams. Add salt and pepper to taste. Makes 6 servings.

PER SERVING: 183 CALORIES, 18 G PROTEIN, 3 G FAT, 21 G CARBOHYDRATE, GOOD SOURCE OF CALCIUM

STOCKING THE PANTRY

A well-stocked pantry is a cook's best friend, especially during the busy holiday season. With the following items on hand, it's easy to plan ahead for family meals — or entertain when unexpected guests drop by. Remember to group foods by categories (pastas, sauces, spices, crackers) so you can reach for them quickly and know when you're running low.

• *Canned products:* Carnation Evaporated Milk; Carnation Thick Cream; tomato and pasta sauces; Libby's Alpha-Getti and Zoodles; tuna, salmon and clams; fruits (peaches, pears, pineapple); vegetables (beets, beans, tomatoes, small potatoes, corn); mushrooms; soups (mushroom, consommé); beef or chicken broth.

• *Bottled products:* olives and artichokes; preserves (jams and jellies); soy and teriyaki sauces; Worcestershire sauce; salsas; oils and vinegars; spices (garlic, dry mustard, oregano, parsley, dill, thyme) and seasoning blends; Maggi Chili Sauce; Crosse & Blackwell Old Country Mint Sauce; Crosse & Blackwell Mango Chutney.

• *Pasta, rice, grains and legumes:* assorted pasta shapes; bulgur; couscous; long-grain white rice, quick-cooking rice and Arborio rice; canned beans such as Libby's Deep-Browned Beans, Libby's Chili Style Red Kidney Beans; chick-peas and lentils.

• *Bread items:* crackers, breadsticks, rice cakes, croutons, bread crumbs.

• *Staples:* flour (all-purpose and whole wheat); pastry mix; brown and granulated sugar; maple syrup and honey; cocoa powder; baking soda and baking powder; extracts (vanilla and almond); chocolate (chips and blocks, semisweet and unsweetened); Mackintosh's Creamy Toffee; Nescafé Instant Espresso, Nescafé Rich Blend Instant Coffee; Carnation Hot Chocolate Mix, Nestlé Quik Chocolate Syrup or Drink Mix.

SOUTH-OF-THE-BORDER SHEPHERD'S PIE

*Make-ahead and filled with cooking shortcuts, this delicious on-the-run recipe
is worth making even when time isn't short.*

Pour 3/4 cup (175 mL) of the evaporated milk into measuring cup; set aside.

• In large skillet, cook beef over medium-high heat, breaking up with back of spoon, until no longer pink. Drain off any fat.

• Add remaining evaporated milk, chili seasoning mix, beans, salsa, corn and tomato paste; cook, stirring, over medium heat until bubbling and thickened slightly. Spoon into 11- x 7-inch (2 L) baking dish. Sprinkle Cheddar cheese over top. Set aside.

• In microwaveable bowl, combine water, reserved evaporated milk, butter and garlic salt; add mashed potato flakes. Do not stir. Microwave, uncovered, at High for 2 minutes; gently stir together.

• Spoon over cheese layer, sealing to edges of dish. Sprinkle with paprika to garnish. *(Pie can be prepared to this point and refrigerated for up to 1 day or frozen for up to 2 weeks. Bring to room temperature before baking.)* Bake in 350°F (180°C) oven for 30 minutes or until hot and bubbly. Makes 6 servings.

PER SERVING: 752 CALORIES, 41 G PROTEIN, 44 G FAT, 48 G CARBOHYDRATE, VERY HIGH IN FIBER

1	CAN (385 ML) CARNATION EVAPORATED MILK	1
1-1/2 LB	LEAN GROUND BEEF	750 G
1	PKG (39 G) CHILI SEASONING MIX	1
1	CAN (14 OZ/398 ML) LIBBY'S CHILI STYLE RED KIDNEY BEANS	1
1 CUP	SALSA	250 ML
1 CUP	FROZEN CORN KERNELS	250 ML
3 TBSP	TOMATO PASTE	45 ML
1 CUP	SHREDDED CHEDDAR CHEESE	250 ML
1-3/4 CUPS	WATER	425 ML
1 TBSP	BUTTER	15 ML
1/2 TSP	GARLIC SALT	2 ML
2-1/4 CUPS	CARNATION MASHED POTATO FLAKES	550 ML
	PAPRIKA	

CAJUN-STYLE BEANS AND RICE

*Short on prep time but not on flavor, this to-the-rescue one-dish supper is ready in the time it takes
to cook the rice. Now isn't that a holiday blessing?*

In saucepan, cook rice according to package directions.

• Meanwhile, in deep skillet, heat oil over medium heat; cook green pepper, onion and garlic, stirring occasionally, until softened.

• Stir in cooked rice, tomatoes, beans, thyme, oregano and hot pepper sauce; cover and simmer for 5 minutes or until heated through. Add salt, pepper and more hot pepper sauce to taste. Makes 2 servings.

PER SERVING: 476 CALORIES, 17 G PROTEIN, 6 G FAT, 89 G CARBOHYDRATE, VERY HIGH IN FIBER

1/2 CUP	LONG-GRAIN WHITE RICE	125 ML
1 TSP	VEGETABLE OIL	5 ML
HALF	SWEET GREEN PEPPER, DICED	HALF
1	ONION, DICED	1
1	CLOVE GARLIC, CHOPPED	1
1	CAN (19 OZ/540 ML) TOMATOES, CHOPPED	1
1	CAN (14 OZ/398 ML) LIBBY'S CHILI STYLE RED KIDNEY BEANS, DRAINED	1
1/2 TSP	CRUSHED DRIED THYME	2 ML
1/4 TSP	CRUSHED DRIED OREGANO	1 ML
DASH	(APPROX) HOT PEPPER SAUCE	DASH
	SALT AND PEPPER	

BEEF SALAD ROLL-UPS

*From convenient prepared entrée to delicious warm beef salad —
in next to no time! These sassy low-fat roll-ups are perfect for two, either as a light supper
or a quick lunchtime bite before the next round of holiday errands.*

1	PKG (230 G) STOUFFER'S LEAN CUISINE ORIENTAL BEEF	1
4	SMALL BOSTON, BIBB OR ROMAINE LETTUCE LEAVES, WASHED AND DRIED	4
1-1/2 TSP	RICE VINEGAR OR WHITE VINEGAR	7 ML
	SESAME OIL (OPTIONAL)	

Microwave Oriental beef and rice according to package directions. With bowl set under sieve, spoon meat and sauce into sieve to drain; reserve sauce.

• In bowl, combine meat with rice and vegetable mixture. Arrange lettuce leaf cups on 2 plates. Evenly spoon meat mixture into cups.

• Stir vinegar into reserved sauce; add a drop of sesame oil (if using). Spoon on top of meat mixture or serve on the side as dipping sauce. Roll up in lettuce to eat. Makes 2 servings.

PER SERVING (WITHOUT SESAME OIL): 97 CALORIES, 6 G PROTEIN, 1 G FAT, 16 G CARBOHYDRATE

ORIENTAL MINI MEAT LOAVES

*The next time supper at your house is a staggered affair, count on these freezer-friendly individual
meat loaves to save the day. Let the hungry hordes microwave them as needed, and have salad or a tangy coleslaw
waiting in the refrigerator to enjoy alongside.*

1-1/2 LB	GROUND CHICKEN OR TURKEY	750 G
1	CAN (10 OZ/284 ML) WATER CHESTNUTS, DRAINED AND CHOPPED	1
3/4 CUP	FINE DRY BREAD CRUMBS	175 ML
2/3 CUP	CARNATION LIGHT OR 2% EVAPORATED MILK	150 ML
1/4 CUP	SOY SAUCE	50 ML
1/4 CUP	CHOPPED GREEN ONION	50 ML
1	EGG	1
2 TSP	POWDERED CHICKEN OR BEEF BOUILLON MIX	10 ML
1	CLOVE GARLIC, FINELY CHOPPED	1
	BOTTLED SWEET AND SOUR SAUCE	

In large bowl, combine chicken, water chestnuts, bread crumbs, evaporated milk, soy sauce, green onion, egg, chicken bouillon mix and garlic. Mix lightly but thoroughly to blend.

• Divide mixture among 12 large lightly greased muffin cups, pressing into cups. Bake in 350°F (180°C) oven for 30 to 35 minutes or until meat thermometer registers 185°F (85°C).

• Remove from cups and serve with sweet and sour sauce. Makes 6 servings.

PER SERVING: 301 CALORIES, 27 G PROTEIN, 13 G FAT, 19 G CARBOHYDRATE

TIPS: *Lean ground beef can be substituted for ground chicken or turkey. Do not grease muffin cups. Drain off any fat before serving.*
• *For a change of taste, tuck mini loaves into pitas and add a dollop of tzatziki sauce instead of sweet and sour sauce.*

MEXICALE MAC AND CHEESE

For the cheesiest, most satisfying macaroni and cheese ever, try this souped-up one-pot
version that delivers appealing Tex-Mex flavor in every bite.

In skillet, cook beef over medium-high heat, breaking up with back of spoon, until no longer pink. Drain off any fat. Set aside.

• Set aside 1/2 cup (125 mL) of the evaporated milk. Pour remaining milk into large glass measure; add enough water to make 4-1/2 cups (1.125 L) and pour into large saucepan.

• Add onion to milk mixture; bring to boil, stirring frequently. Add macaroni; simmer, uncovered and stirring frequently, over medium-low heat for about 15 minutes or until pasta is tender. Do not drain.

• Add soup, Cheddar cheese, Worcestershire sauce, mustard and reserved evaporated milk; cook over low heat, stirring, until cheese is melted and sauce is smooth. Stir in browned meat and salsa. Add salt and pepper to taste. Makes 5 servings.

PER SERVING: 878 CALORIES, 53 G PROTEIN, 50 G FAT, 54 G CARBOHYDRATE, EXCELLENT SOURCE OF CALCIUM

1 LB	LEAN GROUND BEEF	500 G
1	CAN (385 ML) CARNATION EVAPORATED MILK	1
1/4 CUP	CHOPPED ONION	50 ML
3 CUPS	ELBOW MACARONI	750 ML
1	CAN (10 OZ/284 ML) CONDENSED MUSHROOM SOUP	1
3 CUPS	SHREDDED OLD CHEDDAR CHEESE	750 ML
1 TSP	WORCESTERSHIRE SAUCE	5 ML
1/2 TSP	DRY MUSTARD	2 ML
1 CUP	SALSA	250 ML
	SALT AND PEPPER	

PASTA-STUFFED PEPPERS

Talk about speedy suppers! This flavorful, nutrient-packed main dish is ready in just
10 minutes — and all you need are three convenient ingredients. Think of all the time you'll
have left over to write cards, wrap presents, sit by the fire....

Cut peppers in half lengthwise; remove seeds and ribs. Place peppers, cut side up, in shallow microwaveable pan; add water. Cover loosely with plastic wrap. Microwave at High for 5 minutes; let stand for 5 minutes, covered.

• Microwave macaroni and beef according to package directions. Combine with beans.

• Drain water off peppers; fill each with bean mixture. Microwave, uncovered, at High for 5 minutes or until filling is bubbling. Sprinkle with Cheddar cheese (if using). Makes 3 servings.

PER SERVING: 259 CALORIES, 14 G PROTEIN, 7 G FAT, 35 G CARBOHYDRATE, VERY HIGH IN FIBER

TIP: *For a meatless version, substitute 1 package (340 g) Stouffer's Macaroni and Cheese for the macaroni and beef.*

3	SWEET GREEN, RED AND/OR YELLOW PEPPERS	3
2 TBSP	WATER	25 ML
1	PKG (315 G) STOUFFER'S MACARONI AND BEEF	1
1	CAN (14 OZ/398 ML) LIBBY'S CHILI-STYLE BEANS (OR CHILI STYLE RED KIDNEY BEANS, DRAINED)	1
	SHREDDED CHEDDAR CHEESE (OPTIONAL)	

Mexicale Mac and Cheese ➤

THE SUNNY SIDE OF CHRISTMAS

Breakfasts and brunches

are also a special part of enjoying

the holidays — especially

when the pace is relaxed and the

cooking is easy. And that's

exactly what you'll find in every one

of the appetizing recipes we

feature here. From festive cinnamon

swirls to a guest-pleasing

make-ahead Italian strata, there's

no better start to the holidays.

Full-of-Beans Bread (p.65)

ITALIAN VEGETABLE STRATA

*Welcome family or friends to the table with this savory
make-ahead brunch dish — layers of crusty bread, wonderfully melted cheese, eggs and vegetables
baked together in a medley of Italian flavors.*

In large nonstick skillet, melt butter over medium-high heat; cook mushrooms, zucchini, onion, garlic and Italian seasoning, stirring often, for 10 minutes or until tender and any liquid has evaporated. Spoon into 9-inch (23 cm) pie plate, spreading evenly.

• In bowl, beat eggs lightly. Stir in evaporated milk and salt; pour over vegetables.

• Cut cheese slices in half to make triangles. Place 1 tomato slice and 1 cheese triangle on each slice of bread. Place in egg mixture, overlapping pinwheel fashion. Tuck any leftover cheese triangles around bread. Sprinkle with Parmesan cheese (if using). *(Strata can be prepared to this point, covered and refrigerated for up to 8 hours.)*

• Bake in 350°F (180°C) oven for 45 to 50 minutes or until knife inserted in center comes out clean. Let cool for 10 minutes before serving. Makes 6 servings.

PER SERVING: 442 CALORIES, 24 G PROTEIN, 14 G FAT, 55 G CARBOHYDRATE, EXCELLENT SOURCE OF CALCIUM

1 TBSP	BUTTER	15 ML
1-1/2 CUPS	SLICED MUSHROOMS	375 ML
1 CUP	THINLY SLICED ZUCCHINI	250 ML
1	SMALL ONION, CHOPPED	1
1	CLOVE GARLIC, MINCED	1
1/2 TSP	ITALIAN SEASONING	2 ML
5	EGGS	5
1 CUP	CARNATION 2% EVAPORATED MILK	250 ML
1/2 TSP	SALT	2 ML
9	PART-SKIM MOZZARELLA CHEESE SLICES	9
15 TO 17	SLICES TOMATO (ABOUT 2 TOMATOES)	15 TO 17
15 TO 17	SLICES DAY-OLD FRENCH BREAD STICK	15 TO 17
	FRESHLY GRATED PARMESAN CHEESE (OPTIONAL)	

BROCCOLI AND CHEDDAR QUICHE

*Thanks to bake-ahead pastry and a frozen-entrée filling, you can sleep in — and still have lots of time
to delight your brunch or lunch guests with this deliciously different quiche.*

Bake pie shell according to package directions. Place on foil-lined baking sheet.

• Meanwhile, microwave potato mixture at High for 3 minutes or until thawed. Spoon into pie shell, spreading evenly. Sprinkle with ham.

• In small bowl, beat together eggs, evaporated milk, salt, pepper and thyme; pour over potato mixture. Bake in 375°F (190°C) oven for 40 to 45 minutes or until center is firm when touched lightly. Makes 4 servings.

PER SERVING: 351 CALORIES, 16 G PROTEIN, 19 G FAT, 29 G CARBOHYDRATE

TIP: *For a change of taste, omit the ham and substitute slivered roasted sweet red pepper, smoked salmon or Genoa salami.*

1	9-INCH (23 CM) FROZEN DEEP-DISH PIE SHELL	1
1	PKG (255 G) STOUFFER'S LEAN CUISINE BROCCOLI AND CHEDDAR TOPPED POTATO	1
1/3 CUP	DICED LEAN HAM	75 ML
4	EGGS	4
3/4 CUP	CARNATION 2% EVAPORATED MILK	175 ML
1/2 TSP	SALT	2 ML
1/8 TSP	EACH PEPPER AND CRUSHED DRIED THYME	0.5 ML

Italian Vegetable Strata ➤

EGGNOG FRENCH TOAST

*French toast goes festive with a lovely lacing of nutmeg and rum flavoring. For a kid-pleasing touch,
cut bread into decorative shapes with Christmas cookie cutters before dipping.*

In bowl, beat together eggs, evaporated milk, water, sugar, vanilla, rum
extract (if using) and nutmeg. If desired, cut each slice of bread with
decorative cookie cutter. Dip bread, one at a time, into milk mixture to
soak well; drain, letting excess drip back into bowl.

• Meanwhile, in skillet, heat a little oil over medium-high heat; cook
bread, a few at a time, turning once and adding more oil as necessary,
until golden. Serve with maple syrup. Makes 4 servings.

PER SERVING (WITHOUT SYRUP): 371 CALORIES, 16 G PROTEIN, 11 G FAT,
52 G CARBOHYDRATE, GOOD SOURCE OF CALCIUM

4	EGGS	4
1 CUP	CARNATION 2% EVAPORATED MILK	250 ML
1/4 CUP	WATER	50 ML
3 TBSP	GRANULATED SUGAR	45 ML
1 TSP	VANILLA	5 ML
1/2 TSP	RUM EXTRACT (OPTIONAL)	2 ML
PINCH	GROUND NUTMEG	PINCH
8	SLICES DAY-OLD BREAD	8
	VEGETABLE OIL	
	MAPLE SYRUP	

MAKE-AHEAD BAKED FRENCH TOAST

*Thanks to this handy baked version of a breakfast classic, you can relax over
orange juice and conversation while family-pleasing French toast crusts to golden perfection.
Baking makes for easier clean-up and less fat in cooking, too.*

Place bread slices in single layer in large shallow glass dish.

• In bowl, beat together eggs, evaporated milk, sugar, orange juice
concentrate and cinnamon; pour over bread, turning
slices over once. Cover and refrigerate for at least
1 hour or until liquid is absorbed. *(Recipe can be
prepared to this point and refrigerated for up to
12 hours.)*

TIP: *Use a
dense white
bread that
won't fall apart
when soaked.*

• Line jelly roll pan with foil; coat well with nonstick
cooking spray. Place soaked bread in single layer on
pan; spray each slice with light coating of cooking spray.

• Bake in 425°F (220°C) oven for 10 minutes. Turn slices over; bake for
5 to 10 minutes or until golden and egg is set. Serve with maple syrup.
Makes 4 servings.

PER SERVING (WITHOUT SYRUP): 312 CALORIES, 16 G PROTEIN, 4 G FAT,
53 G CARBOHYDRATE, GOOD SOURCE OF CALCIUM

8	THICK SLICES ITALIAN BREAD	8
3	EGGS	3
1	CAN (385 ML) CARNATION EVAPORATED SKIM MILK	1
2 TBSP	GRANULATED SUGAR	25 ML
2 TBSP	FROZEN ORANGE JUICE CONCENTRATE, THAWED	25 ML
1/4 TSP	GROUND CINNAMON	1 ML
	MAPLE SYRUP	

ALPHABET PANCAKES

When it's time to entertain the young crowd, serve up ever-popular pancakes with a delightful fruit twist.
Make the quick mix ahead and store in the refrigerator — for delicious pancakes in minutes.

1	EGG	1
1 CUP	APPLE JUICE OR WATER	250 ML
1/2 CUP	SMOOTHLY MASHED BANANA OR APPLESAUCE	125 ML
2 CUPS	PANCAKE QUICK MIX (RECIPE FOLLOWS)	500 ML

PANCAKE QUICK MIX

5 CUPS	ALL-PURPOSE FLOUR	1.25 L
2 CUPS	CARNATION INSTANT SKIM MILK POWDER	500 ML
7 TSP	EACH GRANULATED SUGAR AND BAKING POWDER	35 ML
4 TSP	GROUND CINNAMON	20 ML
2 TSP	BAKING SODA	10 ML
1 TSP	SALT	5 ML
1-1/4 CUPS	SHORTENING	300 ML

In large bowl, beat together egg, apple juice and banana. Stir in Pancake Quick Mix until thoroughly moistened. Fill empty ketchup or mustard squeeze bottle with batter. Cut nozzle off to enlarge opening.

• Heat greased nonstick skillet over medium heat. For each pancake, squeeze batter into skillet to make alphabet shape. Cook for 2 minutes or until underside is golden brown and bubbles break on top; turn and cook for 2 minutes or until underside is golden. Makes twenty-four 3-inch (8 cm) pancakes.

PER PANCAKE: 72 CALORIES, 1 G PROTEIN, 4 G FAT, 8 G CARBOHYDRATE

PANCAKE QUICK MIX

In large bowl, combine flour, skim milk powder, sugar, baking powder, cinnamon, baking soda and salt. Using pastry blender or two knives, cut in shortening until mixture resembles coarse crumbs. *(Mix can be refrigerated in airtight container for up to 2 months.)* Makes 8 cups (2 L), enough for 4 batches of pancakes.

QUICK BREAKFAST CINNAMON SWIRLS

Surprise the family or overnight guests with these deliciously sticky,
delightfully hot-from-the-oven cinnamon treats. Just don't count on leftovers!

2 CUPS	ALL-PURPOSE FLOUR	500 ML
1 TBSP	BAKING POWDER	15 ML
1 TSP	SALT	5 ML
3/4 CUP	CARNATION EVAPORATED MILK	175 ML
1/3 CUP	VEGETABLE OIL	75 ML
2 TBSP	GRANULATED SUGAR	25 ML
1 TSP	GROUND CINNAMON	5 ML
3/4 CUP	PACKED BROWN SUGAR	175 ML
1/2 CUP	CHOPPED PECANS	125 ML
1/3 CUP	BUTTER	75 ML
1/4 CUP	WATER	50 ML

In bowl, combine flour, baking powder and salt; add evaporated milk and oil, blending well. Form into ball.

• On lightly floured surface, roll out dough to 12- x 10-inch (30 x 25 cm) rectangle. Combine granulated sugar and cinnamon; sprinkle over dough. Starting at long edge, roll up jelly roll-style; cut into 12 slices. Set aside.

• In small saucepan, combine brown sugar, pecans, butter and water; bring to boil, stirring constantly. Boil gently, stirring, for 10 minutes. Pour into 9-inch (23 cm) round cake pan.

• Arrange slices, cut side down and in single layer, over sugar mixture. Bake in 400°F (200°C) oven for 20 to 25 minutes or until golden. Invert onto platter while hot. Makes 12 servings.

PER SERVING: 300 CALORIES, 4 G PROTEIN, 16 G FAT, 35 G CARBOHYDRATE

CLASSIC SCONES

There's no better start to the day than a plate of rich, tender scones served warm with strawberry jam and a generous spoonful of Carnation Thick Cream sweetened to taste with maple syrup.

In large bowl, combine flour, 1/2 cup (125 mL) sugar, baking powder and salt. With pastry blender or two knives, cut in shortening and butter until mixture resembles coarse crumbs. Stir in raisins.

• Combine 1 cup (250 mL) evaporated milk and eggs; add all at once to dry ingredients, stirring with fork until just moistened.

• Turn out onto lightly floured surface. Knead gently about 20 times. Divide dough in half; place on lightly greased baking sheets. Pat or roll out to 9-inch (23 cm) circles. Cut each into 8 wedges but do not separate. Brush tops with additional evaporated milk; sprinkle with additional sugar.

• Bake in 425°F (220°C) oven for 5 minutes. Reduce temperature to 350°F (180°C); bake for 10 to 15 minutes or until golden. Makes 2 large scones, 8 wedges each.

PER WEDGE: 299 CALORIES, 5 G PROTEIN, 15 G FAT, 36 G CARBOHYDRATE

3-1/2 CUPS	ALL-PURPOSE FLOUR	875 ML
1/2 CUP	(APPROX) GRANULATED SUGAR	125 ML
8 TSP	BAKING POWDER	40 ML
1 TSP	SALT	5 ML
1/2 CUP	EACH SHORTENING AND BUTTER	125 ML
2/3 CUP	RAISINS OR DRIED CRANBERRIES	150 ML
1 CUP	(APPROX) CARNATION EVAPORATED MILK	250 ML
2	EGGS, BEATEN	2

GIANT POPOVERS

Crusty on the outside, moist and tender on the inside, these weekend breakfast delights
are heaven with a drizzle of honey. When there are houseguests, make up two batches — one sweet and
the other cheesy (see variation, below).

1-1/2 CUPS	CARNATION 2% EVAPORATED MILK	375 ML
4	EGGS	4
1-1/3 CUPS	ALL-PURPOSE FLOUR	325 ML
1/2 TSP	SALT	2 ML
1/2 CUP	CHOPPED TOASTED HAZELNUTS OR PECANS	125 ML
1/3 CUP	QUICK-COOKING ROLLED OATS	75 ML
1/4 TSP	GROUND CINNAMON	1 ML
	HONEY	

In blender, combine evaporated milk and eggs. Add flour and salt; blend for 15 seconds. Scrape down side of container. Add nuts, rolled oats and cinnamon; blend until thoroughly combined. Divide among eight 3/4-cup (175 mL) greased custard cups.

• Bake in 375°F (190°C) oven for 50 to 55 minutes or until puffed and golden. Remove from pans immediately and serve with honey. Makes 8 popovers.

PER SERVING (WITHOUT HONEY): 229 CALORIES, 10 G PROTEIN, 9 G FAT, 27 G CARBOHYDRATE

VARIATION

• GIANT CHEESE POPOVERS: Omit hazelnuts, rolled oats and cinnamon. Substitute 1/2 cup (125 mL) bran flake cereal and 1/2 cup (125 mL) shredded Cheddar cheese.

FULL-OF-BEANS BREAD

Moist, wholesome and a great pick-me-up for breakfast or any time of the day, this prizewinning,
freezer-friendly snacking bread (photo, p.59) can also be baked into muffins (see variation, below).

1 CUP	RAISINS	250 ML
1 CUP	BOILING WATER	250 ML
3	EGGS	3
2 CUPS	GRANULATED SUGAR	500 ML
1 CUP	VEGETABLE OIL	250 ML
1	CAN (14 OZ/398 ML) LIBBY'S DEEP-BROWNED BEANS IN TOMATO SAUCE	1
1 TSP	VANILLA	5 ML
3 CUPS	ALL-PURPOSE FLOUR	750 ML
1 TSP	BAKING SODA	5 ML
1 TSP	GROUND CINNAMON	5 ML
1/2 TSP	BAKING POWDER	2 ML
1/4 TSP	SALT	1 ML
1 CUP	CHOPPED PECANS	250 ML

In small bowl, mix raisins and boiling water; set aside.

• In large bowl, beat eggs; beat in sugar, oil, beans and vanilla until fairly smooth.

• Combine flour, baking soda, cinnamon, baking powder and salt; stir into bean mixture, blending well. Add pecans and raisins with soaking liquid; mix well.

• Divide batter among three well-greased 8-1/2- x 4-1/2-inch (1.5 L) loaf pans; bake in 325°F (160°C) oven for 50 to 60 minutes or until tester inserted in center comes out clean. Makes 3 loaves, 16 slices each.

PER SLICE: 151 CALORIES, 2 G PROTEIN, 7 G FAT, 20 G CARBOHYDRATE

VARIATION

• FULL-OF-BEANS MUFFINS: Divide batter among 18 paper-lined or greased muffin cups. Bake for 35 to 40 minutes.

CARROT CHEESECAKE MUFFINS

Two popular cake flavors come together in a great-tasting muffin that will have everyone asking for seconds!

In small bowl, combine cream cheese, granulated sugar and 1/2 tsp (2 mL) of the orange rind; set aside.

• In separate bowl, beat butter with brown sugar until light and fluffy. Beat in eggs, one at a time. Beat in evaporated milk and orange juice concentrate. Stir in carrot, raisins, walnuts and remaining orange rind.

• In large bowl, combine flour, baking powder, baking soda and cinnamon. Add carrot mixture; stir just until moistened. Spoon 2 tbsp (25 mL) batter into each of 12 small greased or paper-lined muffin cups; top each with 2 tsp (10 mL) cream cheese mixture. Evenly spoon remaining batter over top.

• Bake in 350°F (180°C) oven for 15 to 20 minutes or until tops spring back when lightly touched. Makes 12 muffins.

PER MUFFIN: 269 CALORIES, 5 G PROTEIN, 13 G FAT, 33 G CARBOHYDRATE

1	PKG (125 G) CREAM CHEESE, SOFTENED	1
2 TBSP	GRANULATED SUGAR	25 ML
1-1/2 TSP	FINELY GRATED ORANGE RIND	7 ML
1/3 CUP	BUTTER, SOFTENED	75 ML
1/2 CUP	PACKED BROWN SUGAR	125 ML
2	EGGS	2
1/2 CUP	CARNATION 2% EVAPORATED MILK	125 ML
2 TBSP	FROZEN ORANGE JUICE CONCENTRATE, THAWED	25 ML
1-1/4 CUPS	GRATED CARROT	300 ML
1/2 CUP	EACH RAISINS AND CHOPPED WALNUTS	125 ML
1-1/2 CUPS	ALL-PURPOSE FLOUR	375 ML
1 TSP	BAKING POWDER	5 ML
1/2 TSP	EACH BAKING SODA AND GROUND CINNAMON	2 ML

CRANBERRY ORANGE MUFFINS

These tangy muffins freeze well for up to one month.

Place Basic Muffin Mix in large bowl. Combine orange rind, orange juice, eggs and oil; pour over muffin mix. Sprinkle with cranberries and nuts; stir until dry ingredients are just moistened.

• Spoon batter into 12 greased or paper-lined muffin cups. Bake in 350°F (180°C) oven for 20 to 25 minutes or until muffins spring back when lightly touched. Makes 12 muffins.

PER MUFFIN: 214 CALORIES, 5 G PROTEIN, 10 G FAT, 26 G CARBOHYDRATE

2-1/2 CUPS	BASIC MUFFIN MIX (SEE BOX, BELOW)	625 ML
1/2 TSP	FINELY GRATED ORANGE RIND	2 ML
2/3 CUP	ORANGE JUICE	150 ML
2	EGGS	2
1/3 CUP	VEGETABLE OIL	75 ML
1/2 CUP	EACH CRANBERRIES AND CHOPPED NUTS	125 ML

BASIC MUFFIN MIX

In large bowl, combine 5 cups (1.25 L) all-purpose flour, 2-1/2 cups (625 mL) Carnation Instant Skim Milk Powder, 2 cups (500 mL) each rolled oats and granulated sugar, 1/3 cup (75 mL) baking powder, 2 tbsp (25 mL) ground cinnamon, 2 tsp (10 mL) salt and 1/2 tsp (2 mL) ground cloves, mixing well.

• Store in airtight container in cool, dry place for up to 2 months. Makes 11 cups (2.75 L), enough for 4 batches of muffins.

Carrot Cheesecake Muffins ➤

RELAXING WITH FAMILY AND FRIENDS

Whether you gather the gang

for a day of skiing or

tobogganing, or prefer to curl up

by the fire with some board

games or a video, you'll find

easy-entertaining main dishes,

appetizers and drinks

that match the casual mood.

Welcome to the relaxing side

of Christmas!

Clockwise from left: Jumping Bean Dip, Creamy
Guacamole, Mexican Melts (all p.76)

HOT AND SPICY BEAN POT

Warm up a winter's evening with this prizewinning supper-in-a-pot that takes just minutes to prepare for simmering. It's especially good over rice or couscous.

• In large saucepan, heat 1 tbsp (15 mL) olive oil over medium-high heat; cook 1 cup (250 mL) each chopped onion and celery, stirring occasionally, for 5 minutes. Add 1-1/2 cups (375 mL) halved mushrooms and 1 diced sweet green pepper; cook, stirring, for 5 minutes.

• Add 2 cans (14 oz/398 mL each) Libby's Deep-Browned Beans in Tomato Sauce, 2 cans (14 oz/ 398 mL each) Libby's Homestyle Red Kidney Beans (drained and rinsed), 1 lb (500 g) diced salami, 3/4 cup (175 mL) ketchup, 1/2 cup (125 mL) dry red wine, 1/4 cup (50 mL) packed brown sugar, 2 tbsp (25 mL) Worcestershire sauce, 1 tsp (5 mL) dry mustard, 1/2 tsp (2 mL) each crushed dried oregano and pepper, and dash hot pepper sauce. Reduce heat to low; cover and simmer for 30 minutes, stirring frequently. Makes 10 servings.

PER SERVING: 338 CALORIES, 15 G PROTEIN, 14 G FAT, 38 G CARBOHYDRATE, VERY HIGH IN FIBER

TIP: *You can use garlic oil instead of olive oil, if desired.*

SEAFOOD CARIBBEAN-STYLE

With a well-stocked pantry (see box, p.53), it's easy to be inventive with even the simplest ingredients. Tonight, why not bring a taste of the islands to the dinner table with this deliciously spiced fish dish?

In saucepan, heat oil over medium heat; cook onion and red pepper, stirring occasionally, until softened.

TIP: *Use cod, haddock, ocean perch or Boston bluefish.*

• Add fish, broth, thyme and turmeric; bring to simmer. Cook for 2 to 3 minutes or until fish is opaque and flakes easily when tested with fork. Gently stir in rice. Remove from heat; cover and let stand for 5 minutes.

• Meanwhile, in 4-cup (1 L) microwaveable bowl, combine beans, tomato, basil, garlic powder and hot pepper sauce. Cover loosely; microwave at High for 4 to 5 minutes or until steaming, stirring after 2 minutes. Serve over rice mixture. Makes 4 servings.

PER SERVING: 441 CALORIES, 31 G PROTEIN, 9 G FAT, 59 G CARBOHYDRATE, GOOD SOURCE OF CALCIUM, VERY HIGH IN FIBER

1 TBSP	VEGETABLE OIL	15 ML
1/3 CUP	CHOPPED GREEN ONION	75 ML
1/3 CUP	DICED SWEET RED PEPPER	75 ML
1	PKG (400 G) FROZEN FISH FILLETS, PARTIALLY THAWED AND CUT INTO 1-INCH (2.5 CM) PIECES	1
1-1/2 CUPS	CHICKEN BROTH	375 ML
1/2 TSP	CRUSHED DRIED THYME	2 ML
PINCH	TURMERIC	PINCH
1-1/2 CUPS	INSTANT RICE	375 ML
1	CAN (14 OZ/398 ML) LIBBY'S DEEP-BROWNED BEANS IN TOMATO SAUCE	1
1	TOMATO, DICED	1
1/2 TSP	EACH CRUSHED DRIED BASIL AND GARLIC POWDER	2 ML
DASH	HOT PEPPER SAUCE	DASH

CHICKEN POT PIE IN A BOWL

This is comfort food with a capital C! Best of all, you can make the filling and bake the pastry cutouts ahead of time —
for a deliciously homey dinner that hungry guests won't have to wait for.

2 TBSP	BUTTER	25 ML
3 CUPS	FROZEN MIXED VEGETABLES, THAWED AND DRAINED	750 ML
1-3/4 CUPS	CHICKEN BROTH	425 ML
1 CUP	CARNATION 2% OR LIGHT EVAPORATED MILK	250 ML
1/4 CUP	ALL-PURPOSE FLOUR	50 ML
2-1/2 CUPS	DICED COOKED CHICKEN	625 ML
1-1/2 TSP	CHOPPED FRESH ROSEMARY	7 ML
1 TSP	POWDERED CHICKEN BOUILLON MIX	5 ML
PINCH	CRUSHED DRIED TARRAGON	PINCH
	SALT AND PEPPER	
	PASTRY CUTOUTS	
1	FROZEN 9-INCH (23 CM) PIE SHELL, THAWED	1
	CARNATION 2% OR LIGHT EVAPORATED MILK	

Pastry cutouts: Using cookie cutters, cut out pastry into shapes; brush lightly with evaporated milk and place on foil-lined baking sheet. Bake in 350°F (180°C) oven for 15 minutes or until browned. *(Cutouts can be stored in airtight container for up to 2 days.)*

• In heavy saucepan, melt butter over medium-high heat; cook mixed vegetables, stirring often, for 2 to 3 minutes or until softened. Add broth. In small bowl, gradually stir evaporated milk into flour until smooth; stir into broth.

• Add chicken, rosemary, chicken bouillon mix and tarragon; cook, stirring, over medium heat until just boiling and thickened. Add salt and pepper to taste. *(Filling can be refrigerated in airtight container for up to 2 days; reheat gently.)*

• To serve, spoon into serving bowls; top each with baked pastry cutouts. Makes 4 servings.

PER SERVING: 604 CALORIES, 42 G PROTEIN, 28 G FAT, 46 G CARBOHYDRATE, GOOD SOURCE OF CALCIUM, VERY HIGH IN FIBER

TIPS: *If fresh rosemary is not available, substitute 1/2 tsp (2 mL) crushed dried rosemary.*
• *For a lower-fat topping, omit the pastry and cut shapes from toast instead.*

CREAMY HERBED PORK CHOPS

Sage and thyme in a delicate cream sauce work magic with pork chops. Let this inviting country supper simmer while you cook the rice, noodles or potatoes and a green vegetable to go alongside.

In large nonstick skillet, heat oil over medium-high heat; brown pork chops on both sides. Reduce heat to low. Add onions and water; cover and cook for 25 minutes or until chops are tender. Remove chops to serving platter; cover and keep warm.

TIP: *For a rich brown sauce, stir 1/2 tsp (2 mL) Crosse & Blackwell Gravy Browning into sauce before pouring over chops.*

• Gradually stir evaporated milk into flour until smooth; stir into skillet along with sage and thyme. Cook, stirring, over medium heat until boiling and thickened. Add salt and pepper to taste. Pour over chops. Makes 6 servings.

PER SERVING: 278 CALORIES, 28 G PROTEIN, 14 G FAT, 10 G CARBOHYDRATE, GOOD SOURCE OF CALCIUM

1 TBSP	VEGETABLE OIL	15 ML
6	PORK CHOPS	6
2	SMALL ONIONS, SLICED	2
3 TBSP	WATER	45 ML
1	CAN (385 ML) CARNATION EVAPORATED MILK	1
2 TBSP	ALL-PURPOSE FLOUR	25 ML
1/2 TSP	EACH CRUSHED DRIED SAGE AND THYME	2 ML
	SALT AND PEPPER	

CAJUN-STYLE SOUP

There's a bit of heat in every spoonful of this deliciously full-flavored soup. Serve it with thick slices of crusty French bread. If you can't find okra, substitute a diced stalk of celery.

1 TBSP	BUTTER	15 ML
1	SMALL ONION, DICED	1
1	CLOVE GARLIC, MINCED	1
1/8 TSP	HOT PEPPER FLAKES	0.5 ML
6	OKRA PODS, SLICED	6
HALF	SWEET GREEN PEPPER, DICED	HALF
1 TBSP	ALL-PURPOSE FLOUR	15 ML
1-1/2 CUPS	CHICKEN BROTH	375 ML
1	CAN (19 OZ/540 ML) TOMATOES, CHOPPED	1
15	MEDIUM SHRIMP, PEELED AND DEVEINED	15
1	CAN (14 OZ/398 ML) LIBBY'S CHILI STYLE RED KIDNEY BEANS	1
1/4 TSP	CRUSHED DRIED THYME	1 ML
DASH	HOT PEPPER SAUCE	DASH

In large saucepan, melt butter over medium-high heat; cook onion, garlic and hot pepper flakes, stirring occasionally, until softened.

• Add okra and green pepper; cook, stirring occasionally, until softened. Sprinkle with flour; stir until thoroughly moistened. Stir in broth and tomatoes; bring to simmer. Cover and reduce heat to low; simmer for 15 to 20 minutes or until vegetables are softened.

• Add shrimp, beans, thyme and hot pepper sauce; simmer for 10 to 15 minutes or until shrimp are pink and soup is heated through. Makes 4 servings.

PER SERVING: 169 CALORIES, 14 G PROTEIN, 5 G FAT, 17 G CARBOHYDRATE, VERY HIGH IN FIBER

TIP: *You can substitute Libby's Red Kidney Beans for Chili Style beans; just drain and rinse the beans and add 1 tsp (5 mL) chili powder.*

TEX-MEX CHILI SOUP

All the popular flavors of Tex-Mex cooking come together in a crowd-pleaser of a main-course soup. Frozen mixed vegetables save on cutting and chopping time — just be sure to choose a mix that contains corn.

1 TSP	VEGETABLE OIL	5 ML
8 OZ	LEAN GROUND BEEF	250 G
1	PKG (35 OR 39 G) CHILI SEASONING MIX	1
3 CUPS	TOMATO JUICE	750 ML
3 CUPS	FROZEN MIXED VEGETABLES	750 ML
1	CAN (19 OZ/540 ML) TOMATOES, CHOPPED	1
1	CAN (14 OZ/398 ML) LIBBY'S HOMESTYLE RED KIDNEY BEANS (OR CHILI STYLE RED KIDNEY BEANS)	1
1 CUP	CHICKEN BROTH	250 ML
	CRUSHED NACHO CHIPS	
	SHREDDED CHEDDAR CHEESE	

In large saucepan, heat oil over medium-high heat; cook beef, breaking up with back of spoon, for 8 minutes or until browned. Stir in chili seasoning mix.

• Stir in tomato juice, mixed vegetables, tomatoes, beans and chicken broth; bring to boil. Reduce heat to low; cover and simmer for 25 minutes or until vegetables are tender. Serve sprinkled with nachos and Cheddar cheese. Makes 6 servings.

PER SERVING: 282 CALORIES, 18 G PROTEIN, 10 G FAT, 30 G CARBOHYDRATE, VERY HIGH IN FIBER

HAM AND SWISS TURNOVERS

Serve these versatile savory pastries hot for a quick lunch in minutes — or enjoy them packed into a wintertime picnic basket for snacking on the slopes. The filling is also delicious in omelettes.

In large nonstick skillet, melt butter over medium heat; cook mushrooms and onion, stirring often, for 8 to 10 minutes or until tender and most of the liquid has evaporated.

• Blend in flour and mustard. Gradually stir in evaporated milk; cook, stirring, until boiling and thickened. Remove from heat; let cool slightly. Stir in ham and cheese. Add salt and pepper to taste.

• On lightly floured surface, roll out pastry to 1/8-inch (3 mm) thickness; cut into six 6-inch (15 cm) rounds. Spread about 1/4 cup (50 mL) filling on half of each round, leaving 1/4-inch (5 mm) border at edge; fold uncovered pastry over filling. Moisten edges and press with fork to seal. Place on ungreased baking sheets.

• Cut 3 slits in top of each to vent. Brush tops lightly with evaporated milk. Bake in 375°F (190°C) oven for 25 minutes or until golden brown. Serve hot or cold. Makes 6 servings.

1 TBSP	BUTTER	15 ML
2 CUPS	SLICED FRESH MUSHROOMS	500 ML
1/3 CUP	FINELY CHOPPED ONION	75 ML
1 TBSP	ALL-PURPOSE FLOUR	15 ML
1/2 TSP	DRY MUSTARD	2 ML
1/3 CUP	(APPROX) CARNATION EVAPORATED MILK	75 ML
1 CUP	FINELY DICED COOKED LEAN HAM	250 ML
3/4 CUP	SHREDDED SWISS CHEESE	175 ML
	SALT AND PEPPER	
	PASTRY FOR 9-INCH (23 CM) DOUBLE-CRUST PIE	

PER SERVING: 616 CALORIES, 17 G PROTEIN, 40 G FAT, 47 G CARBOHYDRATE, GOOD SOURCE OF CALCIUM

NIPPY CHEDDAR SPREAD

This is one entertaining recipe no holiday cook should be without! You can dress our extra-cheesy spread up or down, depending on the occasion, and present it in a number of festive ways.

In food processor, combine Cheddar cheese, cream cheese and chili sauce; process with on/off motion until creamy and smooth. Press into 1-1/2 cup (375 mL) plastic wrap-lined container; refrigerate for 2 hours or until firm.

• Meanwhile, mix pecans with pine nuts; spread on baking sheet. Unmold firm cheese spread onto serving dish and remove plastic wrap. Press nuts into top and sides of spread, patting to adhere. Makes about 1-1/3 cups (325 mL).

1-1/3 CUPS	SHREDDED CHEDDAR CHEESE	325 ML
1	PKG (125 G) CREAM CHEESE	1
2 TBSP	MAGGI CHILI GARLIC SAUCE	25 ML
1/4 CUP	TOASTED CHOPPED PECANS	50 ML
1/4 CUP	TOASTED PINE NUTS	50 ML

PER TBSP (15 ML): 70 CALORIES, 3 G PROTEIN, 6 G FAT, 1 G CARBOHYDRATE

VARIATION

• NIPPY CHEDDAR BITES: Do not refrigerate cheese mixture. Omit nuts. Spread onto baguette slices or crackers. Place on foil-lined baking sheets and heat in 375°F (190°C) oven for 10 minutes or until topping is puffed and just golden brown. Makes 28 hors d'oeuvres.

TIP: *To pipe onto crackers, omit nuts and spoon soft mixture into pastry bag fitted with large star tip. Serve without heating.*

Ham and Swiss Turnovers ➤

MEXICAN MELTS

Amazing as appetizers, and equally awesome with soup or a salad for dinner, these spicy stuffed tortillas (photo, p.69) can be made ahead and grilled just before serving. Serve with a dollop of sour cream or guacamole alongside.

In bowl, food processor or blender, mash together beans and salsa. Season to taste with chili powder (if using). Spread evenly over tortillas, leaving 1/2-inch (1 cm) border uncovered. Sprinkle evenly with onion, then cheese. Fold tortillas in half; press gently around edge to seal.

• Place on greased grill over medium heat; grill for 2 to 3 minutes or until underside has grill marks; turn and grill for 3 to 4 minutes or until browned and crisp. To serve as appetizers, let cool slightly and cut each into 3 wedges with kitchen scissors. Makes 30 appetizers or 5 main-course servings.

PER SERVING: 331 Calories, 15 g Protein, 7 g Fat, 52 g Carbohydrate, Excellent Source of Calcium, Very High in Fiber

1	CAN (14 OZ/398 ML) LIBBY'S CHILI STYLE RED KIDNEY BEANS, DRAINED	1
1/2 CUP	DRAINED SALSA	125 ML
	CHILI POWDER (OPTIONAL)	
10	7-INCH (18 CM) FLOUR TORTILLAS	10
1/2 CUP	CHOPPED GREEN ONION	125 ML
3/4 CUP	SHREDDED CHEDDAR OR MOZZARELLA CHEESE	175 ML

TIP: *Instead of grilling, you can cook Melts in ungreased skillet.*

MEXICAN DIP DUO

Take a break from winter with these sunny flavors from south of the border (photo, p.69). Just set out a bowl of corn chips, put on the Gipsy Kings — and watch the snow melt!

JUMPING BEAN DIP

In food processor or blender, purée beans until smooth. Transfer to bowl. Stir in salsa and lime juice. Garnish with cilantro. Makes 1-1/3 cups (325 mL), enough for 4 servings.

PER SERVING: 117 Calories, 7 g Protein, 1 g Fat, 20 g Carbohydrate, Very High in Fiber

CREAMY GUACAMOLE

In bowl, mash avocados with lime juice until fairly smooth. Stir in green onions, thick cream, salsa and cilantro. Add salt and pepper to taste. Cover tightly and refrigerate for up to 1 hour. Makes 2 cups (500 mL), enough for 4 servings.

PER SERVING: 378 Calories, 4 g Protein, 34 g Fat, 14 g Carbohydrate, Very High in Fiber

JUMPING BEAN DIP

1	CAN (14 OZ/398 ML) LIBBY'S CHILI STYLE RED KIDNEY BEANS, DRAINED	1
1/4 CUP	SALSA	50 ML
1 TBSP	LIME JUICE	15 ML
	CHOPPED FRESH CILANTRO OR PARSLEY	

CREAMY GUACAMOLE

3	RIPE AVOCADOS, PEELED AND PITTED	3
1/4 CUP	LIME JUICE	50 ML
2	GREEN ONIONS, CHOPPED	2
1	CAN (170 ML) CARNATION THICK CREAM	1
2 TBSP	HOT SALSA	25 ML
1 TBSP	CHOPPED FRESH CILANTRO OR PARSLEY	15 ML
	SALT AND PEPPER	

NORTHERN SUNSET

*Here's a delicious new twist on mulled cider that combines the refreshing taste of fruit juice
with the satisfaction that only coffee can deliver.*

2 CUPS	APPLE CIDER OR JUICE	500 ML
1 CUP	CRANBERRY JUICE	250 ML
4 TSP	NESCAFÉ RICH BLEND INSTANT COFFEE	20 ML
1 TBSP	PACKED BROWN SUGAR	15 ML
3	WHOLE CLOVES	3
1	CINNAMON STICK	1
1	STRIP ORANGE PEEL	1

In 4-cup (1 L) microwaveable glass measure, combine cider, cranberry juice, instant coffee, brown sugar, cloves and cinnamon stick; microwave at High for 5 to 7 minutes or until steaming. Add orange peel; stir and then remove. Strain into mugs. Makes 3 servings.

TO MAKE BY THE MUG: Use 1/2 cup (125 mL) apple cider, 1/4 cup (50 mL) cranberry juice, 1 tsp (5 mL) Nescafé Rich Blend Instant Coffee, 1 whole clove, 1 cinnamon stick, 1 strip orange peel, and brown sugar to taste.

PER SERVING: 156 CALORIES, 0 G PROTEIN, 0 G FAT, 39 G CARBOHYDRATE

MULLED CITRUS AND SPICE TEA

Serve this crowd-warming drink in pretty heat-proof glasses nestled in holiday napkins.
• In large stockpot, combine 14 cups (3.5 L) hot water, 1-1/2 cups (375 mL) Tangerine Nestea Iced Tea Mix, 6 whole cloves, 3 cinnamon sticks and 1/4 tsp (1 mL) each ground nutmeg, cinnamon and cardamom; heat until steaming. Steep for 15 minutes before serving. Strain into heat-proof glasses or mugs. Makes 14 servings.

CREDITS

SPECIAL THANKS

The quality of a book depends on the quality of the effort that goes into its development. We have put the best of our team into bringing great food ideas to life for you.

In the Nestlé Kitchen.
Back row (from left): Marilyn Knox,
Maria Couto, Robert Leonidas, Wendy
Parke, Linda Alexander, Kim McKinnon.
Front row (from left): Barbara Lauer,
Sharon Dale, Joyce Parslow.

Special mention must be made of Joyce Parslow, our creative home economist, whose ideas will keep you cooking for a long time, and our tireless team leader, Barbara Lauer.

From the very inception of Kids Help Phone, we have felt a part of the KHP family and doing this project together has been an enriching experience.

Marilyn Knox
Senior Vice President,
Corporate Affairs

PHOTOGRAPHERS

JIM ALLEN: Page 7 (left).

FRED BIRD: Pages 1, 4, 11 (bottom left), 14, 19, 23, 26, 31, 32, 39, 40, 42, 44, 48, 57, 61, 63, 67, 70, 75.

CLIVE CHAMPION: Page 59.

ROB DAVIDSON: Back cover (top right); pages 6, 9, 11 (top left and bottom right), 13, 16, 21, 69, 78.

MICHAEL KOHN: Pages 12, 25, 28, 29, 30 (left), 51, 52, 64, 72.

PAT LACROIX: Pages 7 (right), 41, 77.

MICHAEL WARING: Pages 27, 35, 49, 50, 71.

ROBERT WIGINGTON: Front cover; back cover (bottom); pages 15, 37.

Warm thanks to Jennifer McLagan, Olga Truchan, Janet Walkinshaw and Maggi Jones for their invaluable help during the shooting of the cover.

INDEX

HEALTHY EATING *for* the HOLIDAYS

Nutrition experts agree that all foods can fit into a healthy diet. Nestlé supports this total diet approach. We've provided a sample menu featuring recipes from THE BEST HOLIDAYS EVER to show how you can balance your holiday choices.

According to *Canada's Food Guide to Healthy Eating*, a moderately active woman 25-49 years old needs about 1,900 calories, 65 g fat (30% of calories maximum) and 261 g carbohydrate (55% of calories) daily. Men need 2,700 calories, 90 g fat and 361 g carbohydrate.

SAMPLE HOLIDAY MENU

BREAKFAST

MAKE-AHEAD BAKED FRENCH TOAST (p.62) (1 serving for men, 1/2 serving for women)	MAPLE SYRUP (2 tsp)
	ORANGE JUICE (1 cup)
BUTTER (2 tsp for men, 1 tsp for women)	NESCAFÉ COFFEE WITH 1 TBSP CREAM (1 cup)

LUNCH

PANTRY SEAFOOD CHOWDER (p.53) (1 serving)	2% MILK (1 cup)
CREAMY RICE SALAD (p.25) (1-1/2 servings for men, 1/2 serving for women)	CAFÉ AU LAIT CRÈME BRÛLÉE (p.40) (1 serving)

SNACK

KIT KAT CANDY BAR
(1 regular for men, 1 treat-size for women)

DINNER

SPICY THAI CHICKEN (p.30) (1 serving)	MIXED VEGETABLES (1/2 cup)
RICE (1-1/2 cups for men, 1 cup for women)	MICROWAVE IRISH COFFEE CREAM (p.33) (1 serving)

TOTAL FOR MEN
2,619 calories, 72 g fat, 372 g carbohydrate

TOTAL FOR WOMEN
1,890 calories, 49 g fat, 262 g carbohydrate